Weaving in Brid

CW00906501

(Illustrated)

By Frederick W. Head & Melvyn Thompson

Part I   *Frederick W. Head*
"The Friars" and its memories
a) The Old Grey Friars
b) The Friars Carpet Works
c) The Friars Social Gatherings

Part II   *Frederick W. Head*
The History of Weaving in Bridgnorth

Part III   *Melvyn Thompson*
The Postwar Boom Years

Part IV   *Melvyn Thompson*
The End of an Era

Weaving in Bridgnorth   Parts I & II - first published in 1947
ISBN 0 9529937 4 0   Parts III & IV - added October 2004

Published by
David Voice Associates, 9 Redwing Court, Kidderminster, Worcs. DY10 4TR
Email : davidvoice@waitrose.com

Printed by
Stargold Ltd, Digital House, Stourport Road, Kidderminster

ABOUT THE AUTHORS

Frederick W. Head

Frederick W. Head's father, Thomas William Head, devoted his life to H.&M.Southwell and the Friars Works. He became a Director of the company. He was a skilled engineer and was responsible for developments to the Spool Axminster loom that benefited the whole industry.

Frederick W. Head followed in his father's footsteps and his dedication to the Southwell company and the carpet industry was exceptional. But he will be best remembered as the historian who committed to paper this history of the textile industry in Bridgnorth. Frederick W. Head died in 1974 aged 87.

Melvyn Thompson

Melvyn Thompson's father was an engineer who constructed and installed carpet looms. Melvyn also followed his father into the carpet industry and became the Development Engineer for Carpet Trades Ltd., one of the larger companies in Kidderminster. When Carpets International was formed in 1969 Carpet Trades merged with The Carpet Manufacturing Company and Melvyn took on new responsibilities. These included the Debron process at the Friars Works in Bridgnorth. Now retired, he spends his time working as a volunteer for The Carpet Museum Trust. In 2002 he published his history of carpet manufacturing under the title "Woven in Kidderminster."

INTRODUCTION

Frederick W. Head was my grandfather. When I was a young boy I remember him showing me around the Southwell carpet factory, which, at the time, was part of The Carpet Manufacturing Company. I recall the looms and the punched cards of the overhead Jacquard mechanism and the unmistakable smell of the newly woven woollen carpet. I was proudly introduced to the characters on the shop floor, some mentioned in the chapters to follow. I remember the finishing room with the infectious laugh of George Gower, also the canteen where we invariably stopped for a cup of tea. Therefore, it was a sad day and the end of an era when the carpet factory finally closed its doors in May 1983.

My grandfather's book, started in 1941 and published in 1947, recorded the history of carpet production in Bridgnorth up until the Second World War. Meeting up with Melvyn Thompson of The Carpet Museum Trust presented the ideal opportunity to republish the work and complete the history of what was once a major industry of the town. My grandfather was enthusiastic about the carpet industry and its link with Bridgnorth - Melvyn clearly shares this enthusiasm. The Descendants of Frederick W. Head are indebted to him for researching and writing the final chapters of a story that touched the lives of so many families in Bridgnorth.

I hope you enjoy reading this new edition of Weaving in Bridgnorth.

Robert Davies , June 2004.

REMAINS OF THE GREY FRIARY BRIDGNORTH

Part I - The Friars and its Memories

These notes have been prepared in view of present circumstances, to record as far as it has been possible to ascertain, particulars of the progress of the Factory and many interesting items regarding the early days of the Carpet Industry in Bridgnorth.

It is arranged in three parts :-

a.   The Old Grey Friars.
b.   The Friars Carpet Works.
c.   The Friars Social Gatherings.

The writer wishes to express his thanks to all who have assisted him in any way, especially to :-

W. Lascelles Southwell, Esq., J.P.
T. W. Head, Esq., J.P.

whose intimate knowledge of the Works is well known and covers a very lengthy period.

F. W. H., Bridgnorth, 1941.

a) THE OLD GREY FRIARS

Bridgnorth, proud of its many historical associations, is equally proud of its carpet works - better known locally as "The Friars" a name derived from the fact that the older portion of the works is built on the site of an early Franciscan Monastery.

From a paper prepared by the Rev. Prependary W. G. Clark-Maxwell, M.A., F.S.A., Rector of St. Leonard's, 1913-1928 (Trans. Shrops. Arch. Soc., 4th series, xi. 49) we gather that the Grey Friars must have established themselves in Bridgnorth sometime between the years 1224 - the year in which this order of the Friars reached England - and 1244, as it is known that King Henry III ordered a payment to be made to them in that year.

The first buildings were just outside the town boundary, but permission was given by the King when extensions were made in 1247 for a road to be altered to bring the Monastery within the town ditch.

It may be of interest, owing to his association with, and benefactions to St. Leonard's Church, to know that Thomas Horde, of Horde's Park, by his will dated 11th June, 1498, left the Gray Fryers the sum of 20shillings.

With the suppression of the Friaries by King Henry VIII in 1538, the house was surrendered on 5th August of that year.

An old map of the Town, dated about 1570, gives some idea of the extent of the Monastery.

It is recorded 1720-1731 that "in the Court or Yard of the Convent are vaults underground which run parallel to the house for some space and extend themselves several ways but how far in some places is not known. The end of one of these passages was lately discovered. It resembled the hearth of a chimney with seats on each side but without any appearance of a tunnel. Jars and earthen vessels were also found. The remains described were evidently part of the Friary or substructures thereof."

A note book by Parkes in the British Museum contains a sketch of the "Remains of the Grey Friary, Bridgnorth, 1815." a photograph of which is now placed in the Board Room at the present Carpet Works and a print of which is included in these notes on page 1.

He also states that two stone coffins had been found a few years back in an adjoining garden.

From further records in 1831 we find that the remains of the Grey Friary had been converted into a malthouse, though the great hall, panelled oak ceiling, the stone fireplace and many windows were still in entire preservation.

The Rev. G. Bellett in "The Antiquities of Bridgnorth," published in 1856, at which time he had been Rector of St. Leonard's for 20 years, says that the Grey Friars had built both a Friary and a Church but that the site was now occupied by Messrs. Southwell's Carpet Manufactory. The great hall was then standing and after a lapse of 600 years was still in good preservation.

Nearby a few skeletons had been found, no doubt marking out the situation of the Cemetery which belonged to the Church of the Friars.

It is apparent that the last remnant of the "Friary" was demolished when the next large extension beyond the 1860 factory was made but it is a great pity that no records were preserved of the buildings taken down as the sketch of 1815 appears to be the only pictorial representation left to us of the Grey Friars Convent of Bridgnorth, this probably being of the building marked "Old Malthouse" and taken from the river bank.

Interesting relics have been discovered from time to time and many of the present generation are fully aware that skeletons have been found during excavations for the various extensions to the works. These have all been at the south end, that is the ground at present occupied by the Dyehouse, Boilers and the earliest section of the Jacquard weaving shed.

During extensions to the Dyehouse in 1887, two perfect specimens were exposed which had been buried in graves cut in the soft sandstone. A portion of

another Rock cut tomb was discovered in 1899 during excavations for the enlargement of the Dyehouse. This stone is still in existence at the works. With another skeleton found at the same time was buried a chalice and paten of base metal of the type known as "coffin chalice" thus betokening his priestly status. The chalice and paten are now preserved in the

Stackhouse Library attached to St. Leonard's Church.

Older employees had memories of a "stone pulpit" being in the old Hall and doubtless the subterranean passages also mentioned by them, must have been the vaults mentioned in the records of 1720-1731.

In August, 1927, during the laying of a water pipe, portions of tiles from the paving of the Church were found. Sufficient were obtained to re-constitute four almost complete tiles and the design takes this number to display. They were covered with rough brown glaze and the design was formed on them by impressed lines. Two imperfect half tiles were also found with the impress of a griffin. Complete specimens of these are to be seen in Claverley Church near the Font, at Buildwas Abbey, and in the Museum at Shrewsbury.

There was also a tile of a different clay and fabric bearing the design of the lion passant within a circle. This is attributed to a local manufactory, probably Broseley. These all possibly date from the middle of the fourteenth century. The above have been mounted and are also to be seen in the Stackhouse library.

During the clearing of a portion of the floor of the old works early in 1940, a subsidence appeared to have occurred but on excavation nothing of special importance was found, although a complete "Plain" floor tile was unearthed and there was also a square sandstone block which might have been the base of a pillar. No skeletons were found here but a little farther to the north some remains were discovered in the latter part of the same year.

THE "FRIARS" ESTATE

In 1713, the above estate consisted of Edifices, Buildings, Barns, Stables, Gardens, Yards, Orchards and Banksides, Lands, Meadows, Leasows and Pastures, particularly the Timber Yard, the Great Meadow and the Brink Hill, the Poplar Meadow, the Moat Meadow, the Sling Meadow, the Lower Cony-gree and Upper Cony-gree, Seven Caves used as dwellings, other Caves, Rocks, Pigstyes and specified premises. Early in this year the estate, then owned by Thomas Sheppherd, Ellenor (Elinor) Sheppherd, Will Evans and William Taylor, Chirugeon (Surgeon), was disposed of to Nicholas Harrison, of Broseley.

The estate was held in Trust by the Rev. John Hayle, D. D. Barrow and John Brooke, Bridgnorth, in 1770. The Seven Caves were then occupied by John Beard, James Hagar, Roger Stretton, Luke Goodwyn, Elizabeth Reese, Widow, James Parry and Elizabeth Pool, Widow; while Sir Richard Acton, Baronet, appears to have resided in one of the dwelling houses.

In 1795 the "Malthouse" is first mentioned in connection with the estate so that if this building was the Great Hall of the Convent it would appear to have been converted between the years 1770-1795.

We eventually find the estate the property of Francis Oakes the Elder, Barge Carpenter, who assigned it, together with his Barges, Boats and other vessels and his Barge Building business, to his two sons, early in the year 1817. Edifices were still mentioned but no mention is made of "Factories."

b) THE FRIARS CARPET WORKS

1912

"The Old order changeth giving place to the New" and on this historical ground the Carpet Factory was eventually started. The earliest known references to it are to be found in Hulbert's History and Description of the County of Salop, 1837, and the Rev. G. Bellett's "Antiquities of Bridgnorth, 1856."

There is little doubt but that JOSEPH SOUTHWELL - Freeman of the Borough, 1809, Grandfather of Thomas Martin Southwell, was the original founder of the firm and that later he took into the business other members of his family. Those mentioned below are known to have been connected with "The Friars."

Joseph Southwell	Freeman of the Borough	1824
Thomas Ross Southwell	" " " "	1825
Josiah Southwell	" " " "	1826
William Southwell	" " " "	1827
Thomas Southwell	" " " "	1829

James Southwell, who commenced work before 1832, is the only Southwell to be employed as a "weaver" at The Friars prior to 1840, but as several, probably another branch of the family, were made Freemen during this period it is obvious that they must have been employed at other Bridgnorth factories.

Another family claiming relationship and who bore the same christian names, resided in Hungary Street, now St. Mary's Street, but they were not connected with the Carpet Trade.

The original founder probably resided in High Street, in 1824, but it would appear that he left the district as his death is not recorded in the local parish registers.

Thomas Ross had an infant son die "at the Carpet Factory" on the 26th January, 1827. This seems to indicate that he lived in a house on the ground adjoining the Hand Loom Factory. He eventually resided at Willow Cottage in Underhill Street, and died on the 4th December, 1849. The family was still resident there in October, 1850.

Joseph Junior resided in East Castle Street, in 1851, during which year he was Mayor of the Borough. He was still a member of the Town Council in 1860, and resided in Mill Street. He died on 28th September, 1861.

Josiah left the district soon after 1856 and died at Ham, Surrey, on the 19th November, 1868.

William was still associated with the factory in 1856, as was Thomas in 1852, but these also apparently left the district.

From a description of the Works written many years ago it would appear that at first a few hand looms were set up in the dwellings of the workpeople and that later these were arranged in factories. It is apparent that no factories were in existence at the Friars in 1817, neither are they mentioned in an old rating assessment book of St. Leonard's Parish in 1824, but it now seems possible to definitely fix the building of the first Hand Loom Factory as between 1824-1826.

It is also worth noting that one of the earliest "Carpet Weavers" Robert Trevett, was made a Freeman on 10th June, 1826, and worked at The Friars, while many others were apprenticed to members of the Southwell family.

It is one of the oldest firms in the trade - a company having been formed in 1828 by Joseph and William Southwell trading as ... **SOUTHWELL & CO.**

A small trade card, dated 23rd July, 1828, taken from an undisturbed file containing this and other papers of interest relating to 1826-1834, was found by Mr. Jas. T. Foxall, in 1928.

The earliest record of the factory premises so far obtained is shown on a survey map of the town, dated 1835.

At this date the Company was also operating a Factory on the "Hand and Bottle" Estate, adjoining Foundry Yard. This was demolished, but others were built and at some period between 1835-1855 they occupied two Factories, Offices and Fitting rooms on this Estate, but these had been vacated before 5th July, 1855.

The first type of Carpet to be made was that known in the trade as "Kidderminster" carpet and was usually manufactured in 36in. widths. Later, with the perfection of the "Jacquard" method of selecting the pile threads and its general adoption after 1825, it became necessary to provide larger buildings in which to erect the machinery and this was no doubt one of the factors which governed the erection of the factory. "Brussels" and various kinds of "Venetian" were then produced.

The "Kidderminster" quality was discontinued before 1844 and the two latter concentrated upon.

The weaving rates for the above qualities are detailed on the Carpet Weaving Price List of 1853.

The local firms of MacMichael & Grierson, B. Saloway and J. B. Grierson are all mentioned over a period of years in connection with "Brussels" designs.

In a book containing the work done and payments made to workpeople covering the years 1832-1840 we find many familiar names, the descendants of whom are still associated with the Carpet Works: George, Thomas and John Baker, James Collins, John and William Overton, Henry and William Richards, James Southwell, Edward, John and William Tyler, etc., etc., these going to show how the art has been handed down from generation to generation and there must be many other families whose ancestors were engaged in this trade. Some of the entries are unusual and interesting. At this time many of the employees lived in houses belonging to the firm and it is quite usual to see stoppages for broken windows - probably due to extra-merry weekends. Cash also appears to have been advanced to buy cheese, sheeting, cloth, blankets and calico and for other unforeseen circumstances such as to buy "black" doubtless on the occasions of family bereavement. In one case we see "Payment of Brothers' debt" and another for "Carriage of work." The latter may signify that work was still being done at home and brought to the factory for finishing purposes.

Another member of the family destined to take a prominent part in the works was Henry Foxwell Southwell, apprenticed to his uncle, Josiah Southwell, and made a Freeman of the Borough, 10th February, 1843.

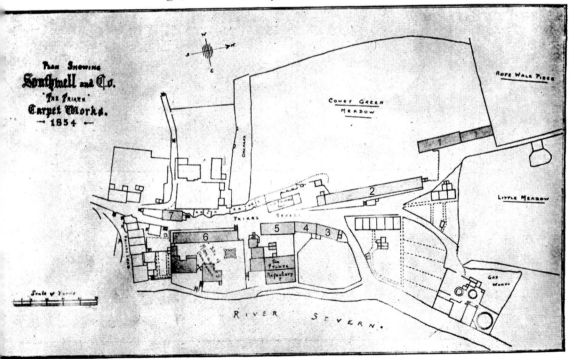

From old plans of 1854, it will be seen that there were buildings, Nos. 3. 4. 5. and 6 situated in Friars Street, as far back as the Sandy Lane, the Old Stove, near the Chimney Stack, No. 7, and also two buildings in Coney Villa Gardens, Nos. 1 and 2, the one opposite the present offices and the other nearer to the Rope Walk Farm.

By 22nd May, 1855, we find that the first five bays of the Main Buildings of the factory had been erected at the South end of the present Jacquard Department behind the narrow factory adjoining Friars Street and covering the site of the Monastery. Buildings had also been erected for Dye Pans, Yarn Drying, Stores, Boiler etc. In 1856, Joseph Junr., Josiah and William were still associated with the firm, as was also Thomas Martin Southwell (pictured right), son of Josiah, but in 1857, owing to heavy losses and other adverse circumstances, it was decided to make changes in the management, Mr. T. M. Southwell and two other members of the family taking control in an endeavour to improve matters, but in less than twelve months they found it impossible to meet their creditors in full.

After making the most satisfactory arrangements possible, the partners getting together what capital they could, pluckily made an effort to retrieve the fortune of the house, the happy result of which will be seen later in these notes.

Jacquard Power looms were introduced in 1858 and 22 looms were accommodated in the sheds erected in 1855. The first weaver on these looms was Thomas Head - uncle of Thomas William Head. With the advent of the Power looms, two of the earlier hand loom sheds, Nos. 3 and 4, were demolished. Thus we have the commencement of the change over from Hand to Power loom weaving. Both kinds of looms, however, were used for some considerable time.

The buildings adjoining Friars Street were at this time used for a Winding Shop, Mechanics' Shop, Boilers, Stove etc., with the Engine Room and Dyehouse in the rear, on the site of the present Cop Winding Department. Entrances were effected by steps from Friars Street and the River Side.

It is difficult after so many years to obtain detailed particulars of any of the early processes, but Ellen Doran (nee Head), who left the works in 1928 after more than sixty years service, at first assisted her grandmother in preparing the warps for some of the hand looms, this being carried out in the upper storey of the Old Stove and both she and Martha Jordan, who will be remembered as an employee in the Axminster Yarn Rooms, many years ago, both acted as "Drawers" on hand looms, the former for her father and the latter for her husband.

In these early days tallow candles were the recognised medium of lighting and were provided by the operatives themselves, while the weaving rooms were heated by open fires.

A plan of the Works, dated February 1860, shows that continuous extensions were being made in a northerly direction and varies from the earlier plan of 1857 in as much as houses and other buildings had been converted into Warehouses, including the "Old Malt House" previously mentioned, and an additional Shed built for further looms and a Starching Machine.

In April, 1860, a new partnership agreement was entered into between :-
HENRY FOXALL SOUTHWELL AND THOMAS MARTIN SOUTHWELL which, respectively represent the "H" and "M" of ... H. & M. SOUTHWELL but in 1861, owing to the death of the former, we find :- THOMAS MARTIN SOUTHWELL *(Mayor of the Borough, 1870)* the Grand Old Man of Bridgnorth and the Carpet Trade, better known to the employees as the "Old Master" in complete control of the works.

It was in October, 1864, that he bought the premises and the ground adjoining on the Old Works site, but did not include Coney Green, so that it may be assumed that the Hand Loom Factories No. 1-2 on the plans of 1854, had by this time, been dismantled.

Edifices are still mentioned in this transaction so that some part of the Monastery must still have remained even at that date.

It may be as well to mention here that the Main Floor of the Old Works seems to have been extended from time to time in Sections of five bays each, and by 1868 we find that the site had been cleared and the second five bays had been completed, the Main Shed containing 41 looms, Packing Room, Mending Room, a space for a further four looms, and the Coloured Yarn Room, this latter being on the river side of the Weaving Shed.

Some of the earlier buildings adjoining Friars Street had also been enlarged and brought into alignment with the three storey Hand Loom Factory (No. 5). The Mechanic Shop, which was then in this section, was converted into a Starching Room and space made for a further nine looms. Adjoining the Hand Loom Factory an additional two storey building contained Card Rooms, the Mechanics' Shop, with a Warehouse on the upper floor, the main entrance and Stamping Room with the General Offices above. It should be pointed out that a basement on a level with the River Side was made under part of these extensions and it is worth noticing a peculiarity about it. Large arched windows are provided in each bay and it was intended that the arches should be built to match the bays of the upper floor. However, some or all of these collapsed, being too flat and it will be seen that small columns were built up in the centre of the windows, an additional set of columns provided and the arches rebuilt half size. This extension included the ground covered by the Great Hall or Refectory, so it is quite possible when this basement was made that in addition to demolishing the last remnants of the "Old Friary" any underground passages then existing would disappear.

Thus we have the completion of the second "Section" of the Main Works, as far as the Jacquard Foreman's Office and buildings along Friars Street to the present Office entrance.

It was at this time that the weaving of "Wilton" cut pile fabric was commenced; three of the first weavers on this quality were Edward Hall, Henry Head and George Maun.

Further extensions were decided upon and carried out soon after the above to provide for another sixteen Jacquard looms and the Winding Shop.

It is of interest to note that originally coal fires were used beneath some of the copper dye vats for boiling the water for dyeing purposes, the yarns after dyeing being washed in the river, steps leading from the Dyehouse under the towing path. Later this washing was done with the condensed water from the engine.

The caves opposite the Old Works were, for a long time, used as Waste Sorting rooms and afterwards, until quite recently, for mechanical spares but their use was discontinued when the soft sandstone roofs showed signs of serious collapse.

On an Illuminated Address, presented to Mr. Horace Baden Southwell, the eldest son of Mr. T. M .Southwell, on attaining his majority in January, 1873, we find that the Works were represented by such well known personalities as :-

W. Westcott	
John Tyler	(Foreman)
Henry Lowe	(Dyer)
Samuel Horsfall	(Loom Tuner)
Thos. Owen	(Mechanic)
John Jordan	(Weaver)

In the year 1877, Mr. Thomas Martin Southwell took the unusual step of paying the creditors of 1858 in full, and thus, after nineteen years of hard work, the plucky effort was rewarded and it doubtless gave as much pleasure to Mr. Southwell as surprise to his creditors. How much they appreciated this action was shown by the illuminated address presented to him (wording shown opposite).

TRADE MARK.
BRIDGNORTH.

It may be of interest to our customers to know that the names given to the following qualities :—

BRUGES, SEVERN, FRIARS, SILURIAN, SALOPIAN, STANWAY, MORFE, PRIORY & ABDON,

are of both local and historical interest.

An extract from a 1931 price list

THOMAS MARTIN SOUTHWELL, ESQ.

WE,
THE CREDITORS OF
THE LATE FIRM OF
H. &. M SOUTHWELL, OF BRIDGNORTH
CARPET MANUFACTURERS,
HAVE THE PLEASURE TO ADDRESS YOU AS THE
SURVIVING PARTNER WITH A DEEP FEELING OF RESPECT
AND WITH DUE ADMIRATION OF YOUR MOST
HONOURABLE CONDUCT WITH REGARD TO THE
DISCHARGE OF WHAT WERE THE LIABILITIES OF THAT
PARTNERSHIP

We are aware that you became Partner in the year 1857, when the firm was considered solvent and that within the space of one year afterwards the contrary was shown to be the case and we accepted a dividend of seven shillings in the pound in full payment of our respective debts. From that time to the present (your late Partner having died in the year . . .) you have continued the business and by your energy, ability and upright dealing have won for it a high character and standing in the trade, and happily in so doing have placed yourself in a condition of prosperity and affluence. No sooner have you done this, than you have paid in full the debts compounded for as before mentioned, debts be it remembered which, under the circumstances could hardly be considered your own.

To us it appears that conduct so noble and so unusual involving as it does so great a sacrifice on your part, should not pass unnoticed and we have, therefore, cordially subscribed to purchase

A DESSERT SERVICE IN PLATE

of which we beg your acceptance, not only as a token of our kindliest feeling, but in the hope they may descend to your children and your childrens' children and be an incentive to them to preserve unsullied the good name you have so honourably acquired.

March, 1877.

Then follow the list of (28) subscribers.

We now come to another important event in the Carpet world, for in 1878 AXMINSTER POWER LOOMS were introduced into England from America by the late Mr. M. Tomkinson, who went to the United States and secured the patent rights for this country. Ably assisted by Mr. W. Adam, we read that the first piece of Royal Axminster was woven in September, 1878.

A Meeting of Manufacturers was held at the house of Mr. M. Tomkinson, on the 13th December, at which were present :-

Mr. M. Tomkinson	Mr. T. M. Southwell
Mr. Henry J. Dixon	Mr. C. A. Ward
Mr. J. Morton	Mr. Henry Dixon
Mr. T. Radford	Mr. H. B. Southwell

The Royal Axminster Manufacturers' Association was formed to control prices etc., and Mr. H. B. Southwell, of The Friars was appointed Hon. Secretary. Members of the Association, including Messrs. H. & M. Southwell, were licensed to use the loom on a royalty basis per yard. Later Messrs. J. W. & C. Ward withdrew from the Association, and Messrs. Woodward, Grosvenor were licensed in their stead.

Consequent upon the above, Ellen Head (left) and Jane Tyler (right), sisters of Mr. T. W. Head and Mr. James Tyler, were sent to Kidderminster, the former to become the first Axminster Weaver and the latter the first Axminster Setter in Bridgnorth.

Early in the following year, 1879, the first Axminster Looms arrived at Bridgnorth and were set up in the section of the works erected about 1870, that is in the portion recently used as the Axminster Narrow Finishing Department and adjoining the present Axminster Weaving Shed. The Setting for the looms was prepared in a temporary building adjoining the Weaving Shed. The first Axminster Tuner was William Woodward, but the Department quickly expanded and additional staff was required, so that in 1881 it was arranged for Mr. T. W. Head to go to Messrs. Tomkinson & Adam, Kidderminster to gain additional mechanical knowledge, his associate at this time being Mr. Harry Young, who in later years was connected with the works of Messrs.W. & R. R. Adam.

At one time the only cart road to the river side from Friars Street was by way of the now vanished Sandy Lane, which started from a point where the Clerks' Office is now situated, Friars Street continuing as far as the entrance to the Gas Works only.

When further extensions to the Works became necessary this lane prevented a convenient continuation of the building programme and so it was arranged with the Corporation to forego this in substitution for the present road, which was cut through gardens belonging to the firm.

This enabled the Offices to be extended, the Secretary's Office with Showrooms above to be built, also the Card Room in the gardens bordering on the new road. By 1882, when a Survey was made, this extension and the greater portion of the third five bays had been erected.

At this time there were adjoining the Offices six houses occupied by workpeople - George Southwell (whose house was eventually used as a Dining Room), Fred Jordan, Tom Head, Albert Baker, Sam Smith and Edward Jordan. The two houses at the bottom of Rope Walk Lane were occupied by Alfred Jordan and James Tyler.

During the latter part of 1886, William Henry Bairstow, who was then manager at Vorwerk & Co., Burwen, Germany, and had obtained a British Patent for a "Double Pile Fabric Loom" got in touch with the firm and eventually arrangements were made whereby he became engineer at the works on 1st January, 1887. Facilities were given to enable him to perfect his invention and get his loom into production.

John Overton, one of our expert Wilton weavers, later went with a loom to France.

On 1st January, 1889, a U.S.A. patent was obtained for it and The Hartford Carpet Co., Thompsonville, Conn., U.S.A. became interested. They appear to have acquired the sole rights to the patent in July, 1890, and arrangements were made for the first looms to be built for them by Messrs. J. Crossley & Sons, of Halifax.

The road along the river side to the Gas Works was widened by the Corporation as a relief measure in 1887, thus making a cart road practically all round the works.

This same year the various properties on Friars Load were procured and according to plans dated 31st August, 1887, arrangements were made to rebuild the South end of the Works.

The Galloway Engine House with water tank on top, Steaming and Drying Rooms and a new Stack were built. The Economiser and two new boilers were also installed and the stoking arrangements reversed, these having, up till this time, taken place from the side next to the river.

The old engine with its rope drive and the oak bevel wheel connections to the additional lines of shafting were replaced.

The club room previously belonging to the "Prince of Wales" Inn, and the houses on Friars Load with the exception of the bottom one, were all taken down. This space made provision for a Starching Shed next to the boilers and a Winding Shed next to Friars Load. There were no basements under this Section - an excellent rock cave belonging to the old Inn actually being filled in.

The houses on Friars Load were at this time occupied by William Corfield, Selina Griffiths, John Head, Philip Rudd, Ben Gittoes, George Tyler and his sisters Jane and Emma.

Coming to the year 1888, 25th June, Mr. Southwell took into partnership his three sons, Horace Baden, Edmund Martin and William Lascelles. In June, 1890, however, the firm was floated as a limited Company.

H. & M. SOUTHWELL LTD.

The Directors were T. Martin Southwell (Chairman), Horace B. Southwell, Edmund Southwell, W. Lascelles Southwell, Wm. Westcott (Secretary).

The machinery then comprised :-   75 Brussels Looms
                                      20 Royal Axminster Looms
                                      with all other necessary equipment.

Plans had also been prepared for further extensions and these, dated 21st July, 1890, arranged for the completion of the main buildings - the Axminster Weaving Shed, five bays being erected with a Basement and additional Offices with further Showrooms and the Board Room above.

The town drain then ran in a south-easterly direction across the works to a point near the Jacquard Foreman's Offices, the greater portion of this, however, was discarded and a new drain made. These extensions meant the demolishing of the six houses facing Friars Street previously mentioned.

Following the above, the room over Mount Pleasant was built for a Drying Machine, but was later used as a Dyed Yarn Stores. Previous to the erection of this the linen and a portion of the dyed yarn was spread out on poles which were afterwards raised into hooks attached to very strong posts and there left to dry. The remainder of the dyed yarn was dried in the stoves over the boilers.

The ground between the existing works and the house at the bottom of Friars Load was also built upon to provide additional Dyehouse accommodation.

In this same year, on 31st October, the valuable services of Mr. T. M. Southwell, in the consolidation and management of the Brussels and Wilton Carpet Manufacturers' Association were suitably recognised, when, at a complimentary banquet in Kidderminster, he was presented with an elegant silver dessert service, accompanied by an illuminated address.

Mr. Southwell pointed out that the trade was an exacting one as it was an "Originating" trade and consequently they had to lead restless lives, giving them little opportunity of taking such repose as fell to the lot of many other people engaged in business, and in thanking them for their great kindness said that in years to come, when he handed on the gifts to others, he wished for nothing better that that the sight of them should stimulate them to increased efforts to promote mutual goodwill and prosperity in the Carpet Trade.

It was about this time that manufacturers produced a new Axminster cloth.

The original looms were arranged to make qualities which were five ends to the inch in pitch, the first, "Royal" also had a heavy pile but competition from America made the provision of a cheaper quality essential and the necessary parts of the loom were altered to make a cloth seven ends to the inch in pitch with a thinner face yarn and a lower pile.

It was decided to make our new quality 7 x 7 with a woollen weft on the back and the first design was completed on the 22nd October, 1891. The more generally adopted "Imperial" quality in which all the weft was jute and which had a beat up of 6 to the inch was added in 1892. The first special design for this quality was brought out on 18th September, 1895.

This cloth, under various names, is still in most general use, although manufacturers arrange the make up in many different ways.

A further quality called "Oriental" was produced on the 15th July, 1895, and in this the pattern was also shown on the back of the carpet.

DISASTROUS FIRE AT THE FRIARS

The next item of interest was on 1st March, 1893, and who of the older employees does not remember that date ?

A fire commenced in one of the oldest parts of the premises the three-storey building opposite the Old Friars Inn and one of the portions originally used as a Hand Loom Factory.

The ground floor was at this time used for Starching and Drying Carpets and it was here that the fire started.

On the first floor were Axminster Setting Frames and a number of Design papers, while in the upper storey Winding and various other processes were carried out and a certain amount of Dyed Yarn stored.

Adjoining this was another three storey building, which also became involved. On the ground floor of this was the Mechanics' Shop; on the first floor Carpet samples and the Stamping and Lacing Department, while the Designing Room was on the upper floor.

The outbreak was discovered at 4 a.m. by the occupants of the Old Friars Inn, but there were a series of setbacks before much was done to extinguish the blaze. The engine did not arrive until 5 a.m., it having taken all this time to get the firemen together, the only alarm being a small bell at the Fire Station. When the engine was taken to the river side it was found that the suction pipe was ridiculously short and would not reach the water, there was also a shortage of hose.

The water mains had been cut off overnight, consequently there was some delay before this was put right, as a messenger had to be sent to the Waterworks. The Works Fire Brigade then found there was not sufficient water pressure.

While all this was going on the buildings collapsed and the whole of the designs covering a period of 50 years, together with the various machinery destroyed, but luckily the wind carried the flames away from the main works. In these, Mr. Arthur Lancaster, the engineer, had cut the steam pipes and only a few Jacquard looms were damaged. The Stamped pattern cards for these looms were stored away from the sections concerned and were consequently saved.

The buildings affected by the fire were rebuilt towards the end of 1893. The ground floor, next to the entrance, was arranged as a Shearing room and contained a travelling Shearing machine for the Hand-made carpets. Adjoining this were rooms for Steaming, Drying and Conditioning purposes. The next floor contained the Press Room, Stamping Room and a room for the making of real hand-made carpets, while the upper storey contained a further room for hand made carpets, Designing Room and Head Designer's Room.

GHOSTS ! !

Now who remembers this little incident ?

Members of the Staff arranged to act as night watchmen after the fire, but an ex-London fireman was eventually engaged. No doubt weird tales of supposed nightly visitors did not lose anything in the telling - at any rate he decided to make his rounds accompanied by his dog. It was not very long before he was made the subject of a practical joke by some of the Office Staff.

A perfect specimen of a skull, found during excavations, was kept in the Offices and this they dressed up and arranged as though reading a newspaper. Open gas jets were in use at the time and these were usually left burning low. As the watchman entered the particular room the gas made a gurgling noise and catching sight of the apparition he made a dash for help, closely followed by his howling dog. "Even the dog won't face it," he gasped, and "Oh ! my helmet !!"

REAL HAND-MADE CARPETS

A start was made in the manufacture of these carpets in May, 1893, first in the old Stove near the stack, then in the portion of the factory rebuilt after the fire and afterwards in the building called Ladysmith. Mr. R. Shergold, Mr. Henstritch and some employees from Wilton were engaged.

Various qualities were produced but the fabric was discontinued in 1901 owing to the greater demand for machine made goods.

During this period what will always remain a milestone in the firm's history occurred, for the carpet presented by the Ladies of England to Queen Victoria on the occasion of her Diamond Jubilee in 1897 was made on one of these looms. It was 18ft. 2in. x 16ft. 5in., contained 4,294,600 stitches and was produced in the rebuilt portion of the factory mentioned above - a room latterly used for Stamping. It took fourteen girls four months to complete the carpet. It had a rich crimson ground in the centre of which was a bold Coat of Arms. The surround, with quadrant corners was on a cream ground. On each side were Rose, Thistle, Shamrock and Daffodil sprays representing the United Kingdom, while at the corners, arranged in oak leaf wreaths and surmounted with the Royal Crown, were an elephant, beaver, tiger and kangaroo, symbolically representing India, Canada, South Africa and Australia. It was on view in the Drill Hall on 5th June, 1897.

A photograph, with the completed carpet in the loom, shows the following girls at the loom: Louie Dunn, Edith Overton, Nelly Shergold, Nelly Akers, Charlotte (Lottie) Watkiss, Edith Broome, Flo Lanin, Ethel Walford, Rose Hayes, Polly Oakley, Annie Shergold, Mrs. R. Shergold.

Of the above, Miss C. Watkiss is still employed at the Works as a Setter.

Many donations were left by visitors who viewed the carpet during its manufacture and these were shared with the employees on its completion. They were also given a tea and two days holiday.

Jubilee Year marked important improvements in the Axminster Department. The Royal Axminster Carpet loom, as originally introduced into this country, was operated with one weft needle only and this had to be inserted three times for every row of the pile, but Mr. T. W. Head reconstructed the loom, patented and demonstrated the practicability of using two or more needles simultaneously so that the time required for the insertion of the wefts was decreased and was no longer a governing factor in the speed with which the carpet could be woven. This loom today is generally considered the Standard loom of this particular class of carpet. Happily, instead of the increased production obtainable reducing employment, the opposite was the case, for the sales kept pace with the production and at a peak period in 1922-23 was 60 per cent. greater than in 1897-98.

It was during the years 1898-99 that further additions to the factory were made.

At the north end another building "Ladysmith" was erected to deal with Real Hand Made carpets, while the Dyehouse and adjoining sections were rebuilt. A basement for the storing of Raw Materials was arranged and a passage made between the Main Works and this reconstructed portion. To allow these alterations to be made the last house on Friars Load was demolished. The Mechanics' Shop, Winding and Starching Department and the Carpenters' Shop were moved to other parts of the works, the Dyehouse laid out between Friars Street and the River Side, adjoining Friars Load instead of between the Boilers and River Side and this latter space arranged for Jacquard Warping, Quill Winding and Wide Wilton Looms.

It was during excavations for these extensions that the Tomb Stone and Chalice and Paten, mentioned earlier, were unearthed.

It may be interesting to record that a scheme to bridge over Friars Load and build the Dyehouse on ground occupied by various other houses belonging to the firm was turned down.

ELECTRICITY was introduced in 1901 for lighting purposes, but its use was gradually extended and eventually the old factory was so arranged that it could be operated in small sections. The machinery in the North Works was driven entirely by electricity.

In 1902 another quality made on an Axminster Loom which has stood the test of time, was patented and produced, namely "Anglo-Smyrna" chiefly supplied in breadth squares. This heavy quality was a good "machine-made" imitation of a coarse hand-made carpet.

Meanwhile, the Axminster Weaving Department continued to expand, Setting for the looms was taking place both in the basement under the weaving shed and also in Ladysmith and to remedy this inconvenience, during 1904-5, Ladysmith was enlarged and connected to the Main Shed by building on practically all the spare ground at this end of the Works. This new extension enabled the Setting, Winding and Threading to be arranged adjoining each other and also made room for improvements elsewhere.

Mr. Edmund Southwell resigned his position on the Board owing to ill-health in 1908. One of the original Directors of the Company in 1890, he was noted in the trade for his colouring ability and knowledge of designs generally. He was associated with the early Volunteer Movement in the Borough and was Mayor in 1895 and 1896.

On the 30th September, in the same year, Mr. Thomas Martin Southwell died at the age of 86, and so passed to his rest one beloved by all who knew him for his cheerful, sympathetic and kindly nature, leaving a gap which was indeed hard to fill. The whole of the employees attended the funeral.

It was well said of him "In every act of his life, privately and publicly he has set us an example which everyone might follow to the greatest advantage." The North Gate was restored to his memory in 1910. Mr. W. Lascelles Southwell was appointed Chairman of the Company following the death of his father.

In 1910, also a number of the employees emigrated to Guelph, Ontario, Canada, and although a few of these returned to England, there still remains quite a small colony of Bridgnorth people.

In the same year, Mr. W. H. T. Harding retired from the Board of Directors, after thirty years association with the Company. He was responsible for the London Offices, but always took a great interest in social happenings at the Friars. He was a successful representative and well liked in the trade.

The firm became interested in 1912, in a Loom for weaving Persian knotted Rugs, and this was perfected, but owing to the Great War amongst other things, this fabric was not proceeded with.

THE GREAT WAR, 1914-1918

Nearly every able bodied male in the works was a member of the local Territorials, who at that time were under the command of Capt. W. H. Westcott, also of The Friars, so that although they returned from Glan Rheidol Camp, Aberystwyth, on August Bank Holiday Monday, mobilisation took place on Tuesday, 5th August, the usual parade night, and this reduced all the Departmental Staffs to a minimum.

It left very heavy responsibility on those remaining and matters were very difficult for a while, but these were gradually overcome. At the conclusion of hostilities, the employees gradually returned home and were again absorbed into the industry. Unfortunately nine of our employees made the supreme sacrifice.

G. Childs	B. Wood	J. Greatwich
E. Head	B. Sankey	H. Smallman
T. James	T. R. Clayton	W. Rudd

NORTH WORKS

During the Great War a start was made to level the land between the Gas Works and the Rope Walk Farm, and by 1923 a sufficient area having been completed, a two-storey building was erected. The upper floor was utilised for the Finishing of all Jacquard products and the lower floor for a Finished Stock room. This enabled the goods to be treated in a more satisfactory manner than under the cramped conditions existing in the Old Works.

Other improvements completed during 1924 was the joining up of Mount Pleasant and the Jacquard Foreman's Office along the river side.

VICTORY CARPET

A special Wilton "Victory Carpet" was produced to commemorate the victorious conclusion of the Great War.

Mr. W. Lascelles Southwell had the honour of submitting this to their Majesties the King and Queen at Buckingham Palace in April, 1919.

The carpet, with a Royal Blue ground and embodied the symbols of Victory, Peace and Plenty, also contained various emblems of Great Britain and her Colonies, together with the respective flags of all the Allies.

The carpet was designed by Mr. H. E. Worthington (Head Designer), who was also present at the Palace.

In January, 1928, it was decided to demolish the OLD STOVE (7), part of the original factory, as its condition had become dangerous owing to the action of the roots of trees displacing the rock at the back. As the workmen were removing the roof the whole structure, with a quantity of rock and a garden wall which was built on it, collapsed into Friar Street. Fortunately no one was injured.

Later in the year, Mr. F. M. Southwell (Director) retired. Before being appointed to the Board of Directors, Mr. Southwell for some years acted as Secretary. On his retirement he and his family removed to Bexhill-on-Sea.

Extensions to the NORTH WORKS took place in 1928-9, a single-storey building being erected to enable Wide Jacquard Looms to be introduced, the products of which also necessitated the provision of suitable Finishing Machinery. Later, in 1932, the two earlier sections of the North Works were joined together and in this portion the new Wide Axminster Spool looms were erected.

As recorded in the Social Section of these notes, the FREEDOM OF THE BOROUGH was conferred on Mr. W. L. Southwell in 1935, and at the same time a Presentation was made to him in recognition of his life's work for the employees.

On Saturday, 15th October, 1938, in the "Microphone at Large" Series, Bridgnorth was on the air. Naturally the Carpet Works were included in the interviews and Mr. F. W. Head gave some interesting facts relating to them.

A novel arrangement of a two needle loom was brought out and patented in September, 1938, by Mr. F. W. Head, which enabled the cheaper grades of Axminster Carpet to be manufactured more quickly and economically, while in 1939, Mr. H. M. Jameson was successful in producing a double width cloth on a narrow two needle Axminster loom, thus enabling a blanket cloth to be made.

LONG SERVICE

Many of the Staff and Employees have long years of service to their credit.

Of the Staff, James Tyler (Managing Director, right) retired after 64 years' service, 1857-1921. His father was associated with Carpet Weaving in its early days and according to Ben Saloway, who resided in St. Mary's Street some forty years ago and whose father was also one of the early manufacturers in the Town, was making Carpets on his own account in Cartway until the introduction of power looms, when he wisely closed up and joined forces with Southwells.

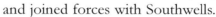
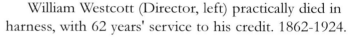

William Westcott (Director, left) practically died in harness, with 62 years' service to his credit. 1862-1924.

During their long association with "The Friars" the greater part of the Old Works was built and the remainder re-built.

Enoch Sargeant (Chief Clerk). 1869-1917. Took a great interest in the Social life at the Friars and the Town generally, being Mayor in 1909 and 1910.

William H. Dexter (Departmental Manager, Jacquard Department) retired after 54 years with the firm. 1875-1929.

Presentations were made to the above after the completion of their 50 years service.

Thomas William Head (Director). 1874-1929. Although Mr. Head retired from his position as Managing Director in 1929, he commenced the building of a Wide Spool Axminster Loom embodying earlier and many new ideas, which were patented. This successful loom was a fitting end to a period of 40 years spent in bringing out many mechanical improvements to Carpet Machinery generally.

A Presentation of a Silver Dessert Service was made by the Chairman, Mr. W. Lascelles Southwell as a mark of appreciation and esteem. The inscription read as follows :-

THE FRIARS. 1874-1929
Presented to :-
Thomas William Head, Esq., J.P., Director, on his retirement after
55 years devotion to the interests of the Firm and Company, by
his friends and admirers in every branch and Department of
H. & M. SOUTHWELL LTD

Arthur William Ball (Designer) 1881 - 1931. Mr Ball worked on several occasions for short periods after completing his 50 years with the firm. His associations with the Carpet Trade is all the more interesting as it formed another link with the past. His father is said to have worked at Messrs. MacMichael's Hand Loom Factory, but as stated earlier, he was apprenticed to Joseph Southwell in 1835. Later, in association with John Baker - who afterwards commenced business as a Grocer at the junction of Friars Street and Cartway - the firm of Ball & Baker was formed. Weaving was done in sheds in Mill Street. Tin pattern cards were used - various hours were worked and at night tallow candles were the only lighting medium.

W. Lascelles Southwell (Chairman of the Company) 1873-1938. A splendid record of 65 years spent in lifelong service for the employees of "The Friars" generally. Always affectionately known to them as "Mr. Willie" he commenced work at the age of 19 and became Chairman of the Company in 1908. Thus ended a period of over a Century during which some member of the Southwell family had been in control at the works.

Records of the employment of youths only go back to 1867 and here we find :-

Thomas Edwards	1867	Dan Caine	1875
Henry Newsome	1869	William Jennings	1876
William Howells	1871	James Foxall	1876
George Collins	1872	William Baker	1877
James Southwell	1873	Henry Preen	1877
Jack Butler	1873	David Bate	1878
Thomas Oakley	1874	Thomas Oakley	1879
William Deane	1874	Thomas James	1879
William Overton	1874	Frederick Preece	1880
Edward Jordan	1875	Samuel Morgan	1880

Of the above, James Southwell, who still resides in Cartway, was apprenticed to the Weaving. It has been mentioned that his grandfather, "Old Jim Southwell" had a hand loom in his own home, but it has not been possible to confirm this. Mr. Fred Preece and Samuel Morgan still reside in Low Town.

All have recollections of many changes at the Works.

The above and many other employees had long years of service to their credit and were well known to many of the present generation.

Of the Staff and Employees remaining at the outbreak of war pride of place must go to :-

Mr. Edward Jordan	65 years	Jacquard Weaver
Mr. Arthur Lloyd	61 years	Winding Room Foreman
Mr. W. A. Piper	57 years	Head Designer

while those mentioned below have been employed continuously for between 50 and 60 years :-

Mrs. M. Lloyd	Miss A. Head	Miss M. Gallier
Miss S. Griffiths	Mr. T. Morris	Mr. R. Holmes
Mr. W. H. Rogers	Mr. H. Head	Mr. R. Baker
Mr. C. Jordan	Mr. H. Griffiths	Mr. H. Baker
Mr. A. G. Griffiths	Mr. H. Overton	

Mr. T. Morris and Mr. W. Rogers, when working as "Half-timers" turned the stamping machine by hand for Mr. G. Tyler when he lived in the house at the bottom of Friars Load. The "Youngsters" with only about 40 years to their credit, hope to lengthen their period of service after the War.

Goods have been supplied from this factory to all quarters of the globe. Agencies were established in Holland, Scandinavia, Germany, South Africa, United States, Canada and Australasia.

In Australasia the Company has been represented for many years by the well-known firm of J. K. Mills & Sons, Co., who have a name second to none in the Antipodes. Messrs. J. K. Mills have Warehouses in Melbourne, Sydney and Wellington. In addition travellers have visited South America, the Far East (China, Ceylon, Malay States etc.). Japan has also purchased goods from Bridgnorth, a high grade Wilton being supplied to a Japanese Shipping Line.

Although the firm did not make it a practice to show at a large number of EXHIBITIONS, wherever Carpets were exhibited they were always successful.

The following awards were obtained :-

Bronze Medal	... London, 1862
Bronze Medal	... Paris, 1867
Gold Medal	... Paris, 1878
International Invention Exhibition ...	... London, 1885
Tasmanian International Exhibition ...	... 1894-5
Exposition Universelle de Paris ...	... 1900
Exposition Universelle de Bruxelles ...	... 1910

It may be of interest to know that the NAMES given to the following qualities Bruges, Severn, Friars, Morville, Munslow, Burway, Stokesay, Norton, Broadway, Dunval, Salopian, Stanway, Morfe, Abdon and Wenlock are of both local and historical interest.

c) THE FRIARS SOCIAL GATHERINGS

The employees at the Friars always regarded as a "Happy Family" were never happier than on the occasions of their Annual Outings or other Social events. Taking first :-

FOREMAN'S OUTINGS

These originated from a suggestion made at one of the parties given by Mr. W. Westcott to the Foremen at Christmas time and although the exact date is not known the earliest of these probably dates back to about 1882, when a number of them arranged to take a trip to WITLEY COURT, Worcestershire.

The following staff made the journey :-

Amos Banks	...Head Stock Keeper and Packer
Samuel Horsfall	...Head Tuner (Wilton Dept.)
Enoch Sargeant	...Office Clerk.
James Tyler	...Foreman Brussels and Wilton Dept.
William Westcott	...Head Clerk.
Joe Price	...Brussels and Wilton Tuner.
Henry Lowe	...Head Dyer.
Thos. Owen	...Head Mechanic.
William Pace	...Head Engine Driver.

The following year the Outing took place to ALKMUND HILL, SHREWSBURY, and the story goes as to how one of the party "stole" several bats from the walls of the under-ground passages and only brought these to light when the company made a halt at Much Wenlock on the return journey.

A group taken in 1885 shows that fourteen made the journey to LLANGOLLEN, while in 1886 a very attractive outing was decided upon. An organised trip from Kidderminster, which was proceeding to Rhyl and Llandudno, presented a favourable opportunity of getting a glimpse of some of the interesting spots in North Wales and so arrangements were made for a Saloon to be attached to the train and for the party, which consisted of the undermentioned, to alight at Llandudno Junction. The outlook was dull but later turned out quite bright exactly what was wanted for a tour of this nature.

Mr. W. Westcott	Mr. J. Tyler	Mr. A. Lancaster
Mr. T. W. Head	Mr. George Westcott	Mr. Thos. Owen
Mr. J. Price	Mr. E. Sargeant	Mr. H. Lowe
Mr. W. Pace		

These were later joined by :-

Mr. E. M. Southwell	Mr. G. Cooper	Mr. J. Matthews
Mr. W. L. Southwell	Mr. Harding	Mr. B. Perry

On arrival a short walk brought the party to the Castle Hotel, Conway, where breakfast had been prepared. After the Castle had been visited, the party proceeded by train to LLANBERIS via CAERNARFON. A four-in-hand met the train to convey them through Llanberis Pass to Bettwysy-Coed, some 16 miles over a road which in those days, was very rough and appeared dangerous, the coach swaying to and fro.

In one of the narrowest parts of the road another coach appeared and what passed between those two Welshmen it was impossible to record.

A call was made at SWALLOW FALLS and then the journey continued to BETTWYS-Y-COED where dinner was served at the Waterloo Hotel. A rumour based on a "message" left for the party that this had been cancelled was thankfully found to be just another little joke.

After dinner FAIRY GLEN received a visit and then the party proceeded to Llandudno Junction by train to rejoin the returning Llandudno excursion, the distance covered being some 380 miles.

In 1887, the previous outing having given so much satisfaction, it was decided to join another trip to North Wales.

Breakfast was partaken at RHYL but the idea of seeing the narrow gauge Festiniog Railway had to be cancelled owing to train difficulties. CAERNARFON CASTLE was, however, visited and later the party returned by train to Conway where lunch had been provided.

26

It was now arranged to visit Llandudno and waggonettes were procured for this purpose.

The weather, which in the early part of the day had been wet, was now very rough and some of the more venturesome got drenched by the sea.

There were plenty of attractions to fill in the time available and Llandudno was left with hopes that further visits might be made, a very enjoyable day having been spent.

What must rank, however, as the most ambitious idea for so short a time originated with Mr. W. L. Southwell, who suggested the outing in 1888 should be made to GLASGOW and EDINBURGH.

Starting from Bridgnorth at 8 p.m., it was arranged for the West of England express, on which a private Saloon had been attached, to stop at Droitwich to pick up the party - supper being partaken on the journey to Birmingham.

Everything went smoothly until Carlisle was reached where they nearly proceeded to gaol instead of Glasgow as their tickets had not been issued to go via this route and despite all arguments special tickets had to be procured before they were allowed to proceed, St. Enochs being reached after nearly twelve hours travelling. Here they were met by Mr. Harding, who was the firm's representative in this area. After breakfast had been partaken at the Queen's Hotel, the party was joined by other friends in the Carpet Trade and a visit was paid to the important premises of Messrs. Wylie and Lochhead, over which they were conducted. The party then proceeded to the Exhibition in Queen's Park. Apart from the usual sections this also contained a building in which had been arranged a large number of the presents made to Queen Victoria on the occasion of her Jubilee in the previous year.

In the late evening, the train was taken to Edinburgh, everyone being glad to get to bed after so many hours of travelling and sight seeing.

Edinburgh was thoroughly explored during the following day - Sunday - and in the evening the greater number of the party commenced the return journey. Birmingham was reached early on Monday morning and Bridgnorth about mid-day. Although very tired everyone admitted that they had thoroughly enjoyed themselves.

Detailed descriptions of these last two outings make very interesting reading.

On one occasion a tour over the COTSWOLDS from Cheltenham to Evesham was decided upon. The Chairman, Mr. T. M. Southwell, joined the party at Broadway and here one of those unrehearsed episodes occurred by which these outings came to be remembered.

A small circus was held up in the town, as the chief attraction, a performing pony, had injured its fetlock.

Many children stood about looking very disappointed when the party arrived on the scene. Finding the tent deserted, the children were invited in, a few of the members took over the band instruments while the others were galloped round by an able ring master.

In the midst of all the noise Mr. Southwell arrived on the scene and was surprised to find that his party was responsible for all the commotion. This was the only occasion on which he joined a staff outing.

CHURCH STRETTON was the place chosen for a visit in 1890 and in a special supplement of the "Bridgnorth Journal" dated 16th August, it was reported that the illustrious party known as the "Foremen's Trip" had duly arrived after partaking of breakfast at "The Feathers" at Brockton en route.

Among other places visited at various times were LUDLOW, MALVERN and EASTNOR CASTLE, WORCESTER and thence to TEWKESBURY by steamer. OXFORD, with a river trip nearly to ABINGDON, DEGANWY, N. Wales, ST. ANNE'S and LLANDUDNO.

In 1924 the early part of a week-end was spent at BRIGHTON, the London Staff joining the party.

On the Monday a visit was made to WEMBLEY EXHIBITION.

Naturally the engineering section attracted the attention of a large number of the party but everyone was also anxious to see the Carpets which had been specially manufactured at Bridgnorth for some of the buildings.

These outings give some idea of the friendly feeling which always existed between the Directors and Staff.

Most of them brought forth some little incident by which they were remembered for many a long day.

The last of these happy outings appears to have been to Llandudno in 1927 - a place which had become quite a favourite with everyone.

MICHAELMAS DINNERS

Another custom dating back about 50 years was the idea of inviting the Heads of Departments to a Goose dinner on Michaelmas Day. Originally a goose was provided from one of the Hotels of the Town but later the meal was prepared at the Works. From these small beginnings and partly due to the fact that the dinner eventually became associated with the Annual Stocktaking on 20th October, it became quite a big affair and included most of the members of the staff. However, with the end of the financial year being brought forward to 30th June, in 1934, these pleasant parties were discontinued.

WORK'S TRIPS

It was also usual for a Works' trip to be organised each summer and these were looked forward to with some excitement especially before the advent of the motor charabancs.

Seaside places were the usual choice, Blackpool, Llandudno, Rhyl, Liverpool etc., but sometimes places even as far afield as Portsmouth were visited. Trips were also made to Shrewsbury Flower Show and Birmingham. London, however, was always very popular as may be gathered from the fact that as far back as 1885 and 1887 trips were run to this great city, and whom of those taking part does not remember the outing here in 1924 when buses were provided on arrival to take the party on a tour of the most interesting spots, each bus being provided with a member of the Staff as a guide. Of course Wembley Exhibition was also visited and it was early on Sunday morning before home was reached, everyone agreeing that they had had a most enjoyable time.

GOLDEN WEDDINGS

One of the occasions when the "Happy Family" feeling existing at "The Friars" was expressed was on 17th September, 1900, the Golden Wedding Anniversary of
MR. AND MRS. T. M. SOUTHWELL
then residing at Fairfield, Oldbury, when besides adding their congratulations to the many others which poured in "Everyone" at the Works subscribed towards a portrait painting of Mr. Southwell as a GOLDEN WEDDING PRESENT.

Wilfred Von Glehn, an artist of considerable ability, was commissioned to carry out the work and the presentation took place on Saturday, 1st December of the same year in the Drill Hall.

The Committee responsible for carrying out the arrangements were :-

Mr. E. Sargeant	...	...	...	... Staff
Mr. W. H. Westcott	...	...	...	... Staff
Mr. J. Matthews	...	...	...	... Designer

Messrs. J. Tyler, W. Dexter,	...	...	... |
W. Richards, J. Jones, E. Hall, ...	...	... | Brussels Department
A. Lancaster, A. E. Jordan, J. Overton ...	...	... | and
Misses A. Oakley, Rowlands, Tyler	...	... | General Employees
Mrs. Gittoes, Mrs. Jordan	...	...	... |

Mr. T. W. Head	...	...	... ... |
Mrs. J. Jenkins, Mrs. E. Winwood	...	... | Axminster
Miss Gallier, Miss E. Fewtrell ...	...	... | Department
Mrs. Shergold	...	...	... ... |

Selections were played by the Town Band under Band Master J. Davies and a short musical programme was also carried out.

The presentation was made by Mr. Wm. Westcott, while representatives of the various departments added their congratulations. Mr. T. M. Southwell, in thanking everyone for their kindness in arranging the meeting at the Drill Hall, and for the singular beauty of the present, spoke of the perfect harmony between the employees and himself and mentioned that this was the second Golden Wedding at the Friars during the year as Mr. Edwin Head and his wife celebrated their's on 29th October.

He also said that at one time he had four generations of one family at work at the same time.

PEACE CELEBRATIONS

Soon after the Great War, 1914-1918, rumours of a Re-union were in the air - that is a party at the Hundred House - that's where many jolly times had been spent.

This was not the original meeting place, however, as older employees remember the time nearly 50 years ago, when the various departments arranged their own separate New Year teas, these taking place in the club rooms of the Hotels of the town, "Squirrel", "King's Head", "The Old Friars" etc., and it was here on one occasion that the lights suddenly went out and a "ghostly spirit" appeared reciting :- "I am a Friar of Orders Grey , Who lived in a Friary over the way ..." and that was about as far as the recitation got for one of the party, not in the know, threw the nearest thing to hand, the "ghost" and the dish of flaming "spirit" soon being scattered.

These separate sections were eventually united and a combined Tea and Dance was held for many years in the Agricultural Hall soon after the Christmas Holidays.

It was customary, in the summer, for many of the employees to assist Mr. T. W. Head at children's parties on the Hundred House bowling green and these usually brighter outdoor fetes were so attractive that the works' parties were eventually held there during the summer months.

It was on 26th July, 1919, that the Works' "Peace" celebrations were held, commencing with a Carnival Procession to the Hundred House, where Sports, Tea and Dancing took place.

What a Carnival ! but it was the forerunner of even better. The outstanding feature was the Jazz Band, under the conductorship of Mr. E. Felton, and this must have been one of the earliest bands of its kind. The town was crowded with people to see the return procession.

NORTH WORKS

It was on 29th December, 1923, that the opening of the new extensions adjoining the Gas Works was marked by an Illuminated Fancy Dress parade from the Drill Hall to the Works, where a Dance and Entertainment which included items by the Male Voice choir took place. Another, quite different, but memorable party.

LONG SERVICE CELEBRATIONS

On the 16th June, 1923, the whole of the employees, including the London Staff, Australian and other representatives, made a trip to Blackpool, the occasion being the presentation to Mr. W. Lascelles Southwell (right), Chairman of the Company, to mark his 50 years with the firm.

The presentation, made by Major W. H. Westcott, took the form of an Oil Painting, by Mr. A. Chevallier Taylor, together with an Illuminated Address in album form.

Mr. Southwell, in acknowledging the present, made one of his happy remarks "I knew I was going to be presented with the painting because I sat for it, but the album is a great surprise." He also mentioned that business had increased four-fold since he joined the firm.

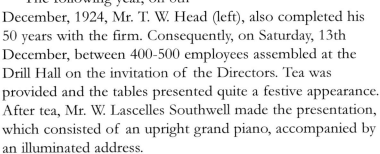

The following year, on 8th December, 1924, Mr. T. W. Head (left), also completed his 50 years with the firm. Consequently, on Saturday, 13th December, between 400-500 employees assembled at the Drill Hall on the invitation of the Directors. Tea was provided and the tables presented quite a festive appearance. After tea, Mr. W. Lascelles Southwell made the presentation, which consisted of an upright grand piano, accompanied by an illuminated address.

Commencing as a half timer before he was ten years of age, Mr. Head worked first in the Stamping room and then as a creeler. At the age of 16 he spent a short time at the Works of Messrs. Tomkinson and Adam, Kidderminster, so as to become better acquainted with the mechanism of the Royal Axminster Carpet Loom, eventually taking charge of the Axminster Department when he was only eighteen.

He said he hoped the younger generation might see that it was quite possible to lead good and useful lives and win golden opinions from their fellow workers without being born with silver spoons in their mouths.

The name of Southwell stood in a high and honourable position in the carpet trade and they must keep it there. They could not stand still - there must be continual progress.

Be not content with the former worth - Stand fast ! Look forward ! Persevering to the last - from well to better and there would be no fear for the future of the Friars.

In the following year, 1925, Mr. and Mrs. T. W. Head invited the employees to tea at the Friars and in conjunction with this excellent Carnival procession paraded from the Cricket Field through the town to the Works, attracting large crowds from whom a collection in aid of the Bridgnorth Infirmary was made, and amounted to £130 0s. 0d.

On the 27th July, 1929, to mark his retirement, Mr. T. W. Head again invited all the employees and pensioners to a Social Gathering in the fields adjoining the North Works. Maypole and Country Dancing were special features of the afternoon programme, which also included dancing, community singing and sports.

FREEDOM OF THE BOROUGH

A day that must for ever live in the memory of those fortunate enough to be present was Wednesday, 9th October, 1935, when the Honorary Freedom of the Borough was conferred on the Chairman.

The Silver casket bore on its lid the Borough Arms, while in the front were the intertwined initials "W.L.S." The parchment scroll was beautifully worked - on the left was the Borough Arms and on the right the seal of the Council, over which were the words :-

"Given under the common seal of the Mayor,
Aldermen and Burgesses of the Borough of Bridgnorth."

In the centre part of the scroll were the following words :-

"BOROUGH OF BRIDGNORTH"

At a meeting of the Town Council of the Borough of Bridgnorth, convened in accordance with the provisions of the Local Government Act, 1933, and held at the Town Hall, in the said Borough, the ninth day of October, 1935.
It was unanimously resolved :-
That this Council do hereby confer upon :-
WILLIAM LASCELLES SOUTHWELL, ESQUIRE, Justice of Peace of the Borough of Bridgnorth and of the County of Salop, the Honorary Freedom of the Borough of Bridgnorth, the most honourable distinction which it is their privilege to bestow, in recognition of the eminent services rendered by him to the Borough.

THIS IS TO CERTIFY that William Lascelles Southwell, Esquire, J.P., has been duly sworn and admitted to the Honorary Freedom of the Borough pursuant to the above resolution.

This was signed by the Mayor and Town Clerk.

In the evening, as the occasion demanded, His Worship the Mayor, Aldermen, Councillors and Borough Officials, The Management Committee and Staff of the Bridgnorth and South Shropshire Infirmary, the whole of the Employees and Pensioners from the Works were invited to tea at the Drill Hall. The party also being in celebration of Mr. Southwell's 80th birthday.

Mr. H. M. Jameson spoke of the respect in which Mr. Southwell was held throughout the whole of the Carpet Trade, both among his fellow Manufacturers and the Company's customers, but especially so by the Staff, Representatives and Employees, to whom he was known as Mr. Willie.

The Mayor said "As leader in our industrial life, he has been the one man who has been mainly responsible for the very existence of the Friars Carper Works, which has given employment to hundreds of our men and women over many years, but even with so busy a life, industrially he has found time to give wonderful service to the public and in many other ways."

After the presentation of a cheque by two of the oldest employees, Mr. W. Overton and Miss M. Gallier, in recognition of his life's work for the employees, Mr. Southwell handed the cheque over to the Infirmary, a bed in the men's ward being named after him.

With a concert and dancing, a most notable day was brought to a close.

FAREWELL PRESENTATION

As already recorded, Mr. W. L. Southwell moved from Bridgnorth to Milford-on-Sea on his retirement, and so later in the same year - 25th September, 1938 - a happy re-union took place when ...

Colonel H. L. Oldham	*Chairman.*	Mr. W. S. Collins
Mr. H. Mellor Jameson	*Managing Director*	Mr. H. Overton
Mr. Frederick W. Head	*Works Manager*	Mr. W. Rogers
Mr. W. A. Piper		Mr. E. Crockson

... called on Mr. Southwell in his new home.

On this occasion the party travelled by road - quite a pleasant change from the usual practice. The country was new to many. A stop was made for tea at Marlborough and the journey then continued to Bournemouth.

On the Sunday morning an early start was made for Milford-on-Sea.

Naturally Mr. Southwell was very glad to see some of his old comrades and employees and they just as pleased to see him.

Colonel H. L. Oldham made a presentation, which consisted of two Volumes of a book and a third Volume containing a short farewell address, personally signed by the Directors and representatives of the Staff and Workpeople.

Lunch was kindly provided by Mr. Southwell and all too soon the journey home had to be commenced. Cheltenham was the calling place for tea and Bridgnorth reached in the evening.

As events turned out this proved to be the last of the Social Gatherings for the present and what a host of happy memories they have left behind.

CONCLUSION

But again the "OLD order changeth, giving place to the NEW" for with the outbreak of war and in anticipation of reduced requirements it was decided to confine the manufacturing plant in the North Works as far as possible and when part of the main Jacquard Weaving Shed was cleared in 1939 a certain number of the narrow looms were transferred to these Works. The remainder of the Jacquard Weaving Shed was eventually cleared by August, 1940, as this part of the Old Works had been sub-let.

However, in October, 1940, the North Works, together with the remainder of the Old Works, were earmarked for more important national work.

The manufacture of Axminster Carpet ceased on the 4th of November, and Wilton Carpet on the 12th November, 1940, a few Axminster looms continuing to make blanket cloth until early in 1941; and so for the first time for well over 100 years the manufacture of carpet has ceased in Bridgnorth. However, by the kindly assistance of fellow manufacturers in Kidderminster, existing designs in all qualities were still produced and thus the good name of the firm went on.

Most of the workpeople will find other interesting employment for the period of the war, but CARPETS are still foremost in their thoughts and all long for the time when they will be able to return to their normal work and so for the present we must leave "THE FRIARS AND ITS MEMORIES."

ADDENDUM
FLOODS

An exceptional flood occurred on Sunday, 10th February, 1946, the water reaching a depth of over six inches in the North Works and 1ft. 6in. in the basement of the Old Works. The water receded during Sunday night, but it was not possible to commence production again until Thursday, 14th February. No one connected with the works has any recollection of water having reached the basement of the Old Works during their lifetime.

On Saturday, 22nd March, 1947, an even greater flood occurred. On this occasion the water rose to over ten inches in the North Works, but fortunately the water cleared during the night and the Works were soon in production again.

SOUTHWELL & CO.,
THE FRIARS CARPET WORKS, BRIDGNORTH.

WEAVERS

During the period 11th August, 1832 to 18th January, 1840.

Allen, Jas.

Brooks, William
Banner, James
Beach, Joseph
Baker, Thomas
Brazier, Henry
Barker, Thomas
Biddle, Thomas
Bradley, Thomas
Bayley, John
Barker, John
Brown, William
Baker, John
Baker, George
Brumage, John
Barker, George

Charlton, Joseph
Ciddall, Thomas
Collins, James
Climer, Charles
Crowther, William
Cale, George
Castree, James
Cookson, Richard
Cookson, Samuel

Davis, John
Dalaway, John
Deighton, John

Elcock. Jacob
Ecob, Edwin
Eurskine, John
Evans, John
Evans, Thomas

Fosbrook, James
Feriday, Josiah

Green, Josiah
Gwynn, Thomas
Guise, Benjamin
Giddins, John
Gregory, William
Gittins, Thomas

Hayes, John
Harman, John
Harman, William
Harman, Charles
Horton, Solomon
Hopkins, Thomas

Hall, William
Hill, Samuel
Hampton, Richard
Harding, Thomas
Hall, William
Hickman, John
Hill, Thomas
Hardiman, James
Hill, John
Heritage, John
Henley, John
Hill, Joseph
Hatten, William
Hebblethwaite, Joseph
Hebblethwaite, John
Hayward, John
Hughes, William

Jevons, William
Jordan, Benjamin

Kitching, Richard

Law, William
Lee, William
Lee, Richard
Lines, Samuel

Martin, John
Medes, John
Mills, James
Medes, William
Martin, Henry
Maund, James

Newey, William

Overton, John
Overton, William

Pagett, William
Partridge, William
Pickin, Thomas
Preene, Thomas
Parler, William
Perrins, Benjamin
Paget, John
Payne, William
Pearsall, Benjamin
Pugh, Benjamin

Roberts, Thomas
Richards, William
Raymond, John

Reynolds, Thomas
Robinson, William
Richards, Henry
Rutter, James
Roberts, Thomas

Smith, John
Shipman, John
Southall, John
Southwell, James
Shipman, Henry
Shipman, John (Senr.)
Sanger, Charles
Smith, John
Shepherd, John
Smith, Thomas
Slater, Henry
Starr, Nathaniel
Stephens, Richard
Stooke, Alfred
Stainer, George
Summers, Francis
Smith, William

Thomas, Joseph
Taylor, John
Tunington, John
Trevitt, William
Tonkiss, William
Trevitt, Aaron
Tyler, John
Tyler, William
Tolley, James
Tolley, Henry
Tennant, John
Thrasher, William
Trevitt, Robert
Tidman, James
Tyler, Edward

Vale, Edward

Woosnam, John
Walker, William
Wylde, William
Walden, Thomas
Warman, George
Walford, Richard
Wilks, William
Wright, Edward
Wakefield, Thomas
Wilson, Benjamin

Yates, Richard

W. A. Piper   J. Lowe   A. W. Ball

Designing Room, 1912

Axminster Setting, 1912

Section of Axminster Weaving Shed, 1912

Section of Jacquard Weaving Shed, 1912

Finishing Room, 1912

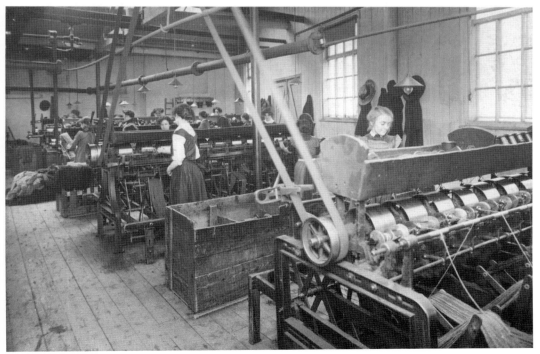

Winding Room, 1912

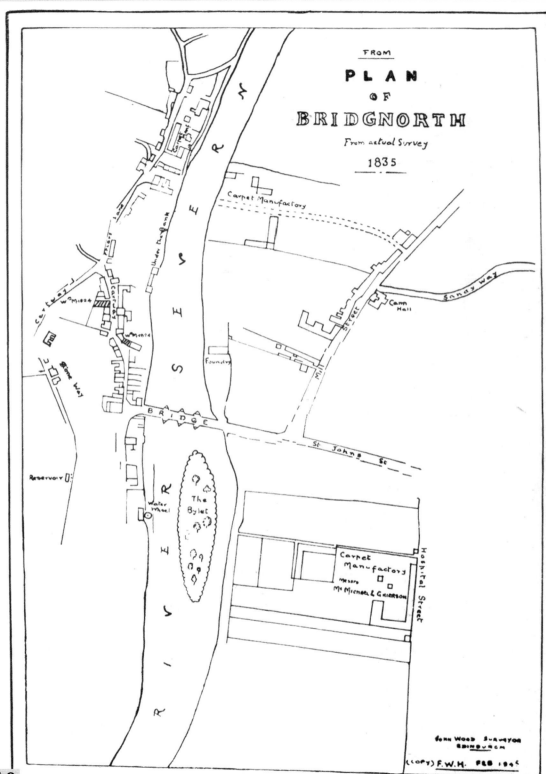

FROM

PLAN

OF

BRIDGNORTH

From actual Survey

1835

JOHN WOOD SURVEYOR
EDINBURGH

(COPY) F.W.H. FEB 1945

Part II - The History of Weaving in Bridgnorth

A paper read to the Bridgnorth and District Historical Society
on 2nd December, 1946.

Bridgnorth, 1946.

The writer expresses his thanks to the many who have provided information which has enabled him to prepare the following paper, especially to :-

Dr. Watkins Pitchford
Mr. E. H. Pee
Mr. H. R. Foxall
Mr. Ben Saloway (Canada)

and hopes that it will serve as a record of the Weaving Industry in the Borough.

WEAVING IN BRIDGNORTH

It is difficult to say just when the "Art" of weaving commenced in Bridgnorth, but the antiquity of the cloth trade in the County of Shropshire as a whole is attested by various references in ancient records to the neglect of certain towns and boroughs to keep the Assize of Cloth. In 1203 it was reported that the town had failed to keep this assize, a failure which rendered it liable to a fine, fixed in this case at four marks.

In 1223, the burgesses having complained that those of Shrewsbury would not allow them to buy undressed cloth or raw hides in their markets, a jury was empanelled on 25th November of that year at Westminster to try the cause, the right of Shrewsbury to so refuse being fully established. It is possible, therefore, that Bridgnorth had more facilities for finishing cloth than was required for dealing with that produced by the local weavers and that they were endeavouring to obtain additional supplies from outside to keep this particular section fully employed.

There were apparently two types - Strong Cloth 7/8 yard wide and Small Cloth slightly narrower. Welch farm house cloth at this time sold at 16d. to 17d. per yard. The average price for all cloths being 14d. per yard. In these early days much of the cloth was exported to the continent, sometimes being dyed beforehand.

A charter was granted to the Borough as far back as 20th June, 1227, in the reign of Henry III, whereby it had the privilege of establishing a Guild or Hanse, i.e. of building a Guild Hall and establishing Traders Guilds to which all trades people, etc. of the Borough had to be members. Some of these Guilds or Companies lingered on into the 18th Century.

41

In 1505 the Bailiffs and Burgesses ordered that no "northern man" should bring any northern cloth "being whytis" to town to sale for two years, whether this was a first indication of a falling off in trade it is difficult to say, but the weaving of cloth was no doubt the staple industry of the town about this time, as Leland, writing about 1530 says "The Towne stondithe by Clothinge, and that now decayed there, the Towne sorely decayeth therewith."

The industry, however, must have had another successful period as the "Company of Cappers" flourished prior to 1571. During this year, in the reign of Queen Elizabeth, an Act of Parliament was passed to enforce the wearing of Woollen Caps, but this failing to have the desired effect the Queen thought fit to exert her Royal Prerogative in the matter, and issued a proclamation for the purpose of enforcing the statute, compelling everyone in her Realm, except the nobility, to wear woollen caps, as the violation of the Act of Parliament tended "to the decay, ruin, and desolation of divers Antient Cities and Boroughs which had been the nourishers and bringers up in that faculty, of great numbers of people, as London, also Exeter, Bristol, Monmouth, Hereford, Rosse and Bridgnorth." These caps were called "Statute" caps.

It is not possible to say when the "Weavers" etc. Guild (and by this etc. it may mean any trade associated with weaving) was formed, or how long it remained in existence, but there are records of two civil actions on their behalf between November, 1713 and February, 1753.

14th July, 1718

23rd October, 1719

In these actions John Fields, Warden of the Society of Weavers sued on their behalf and it will be seen that he was one of the earliest weavers to be made a Freeman of the Borough.

The first weaver to be mentioned is William Smith, Haughton, 11th March 1661, and while many other weavers were made Freemen these can hardly be said to represent the extent of the Cloth Weaving Industry of the Town, but doubtless when Carpet Weaving was introduced Cloth Weavers would be attracted to this new Art.

There does not appear to be any record of Factories for Cloth Weaving or Finishing, although many local residents still have recollections of a man named Roberts weaving "Sacking" and similar fabrics in the house now occupied by Mr. W. Rogers, 11, Listley Street.

Thomas Roberts was a Twine and Rope Manufacturer in Listley Street in 1851, and it is possible that he made the necessary weft for the sacking which was woven.

Owing to the depression Cloth weaving ceased at Shrewsbury in 1817, and there seems little doubt but that cloth weaving generally ceased in Bridgnorth soon after the introduction of carpets.

It has been suggested that their introduction was due to a great strike at Kidderminster, then the centre of the Carpet Industry, but as this did not take place until 1828, it is obvious that this was not the case, although a few weavers migrated from that district and were made Freemen of the Borough.

The first persons mentioned in connection with Carpets in the Borough Records are :-

John Broome	Kidderminster	Carpet Weaver, 7th July, 1769
Joseph MacMichael	Bridgnorth	Carpet Manufacturer, 21st July, 1802
Joseph Southwell	Bridgnorth	Carpet Weaver, 4th December, 1809

The two latter were destined to take a leading part in developing this Industry in the town.

The MacMichael Family are of Scottish origin and came from some part of Galloway or Dumfriesshire, while the Southwell family are said to originate from Worcestershire.

The weaving of Carpets is understood to have originally been a "Home" product in the town, but at the same time it will be seen from the following references that a factory, probably the first, was established in Listley Street by Joseph MacMichael at the latter part of the 18th or at the commencement of the 19th century.

Entries in the Register of Stoneway Chapel seem to indicate that a family of this name came to Bridgnorth in 1797 and as he was described as a Carpet Manufacturer in 1802, when he was made a Freeman of the Borough, the factory was probably started between those dates.

In a manuscript by William Hardwick, 1772-1843, "Collections for a History of Bridgnorth" and published by Dr. Watkins Pitchford in 1938, we find Tainter Hill and Tainter Wall referred to as being associated with the Weaving Industry.

Of the former we read, "these sloping grounds, now gardens between Listley Street and Hollybush Road, are marked Tenter Yard on an estate map of 1777, a name doubtless due to their being used for the 'Tentering' i.e. stretching of freshly woven woollen material." This term was also used where linen cloth was stretched out and exposed for bleaching purposes.

It is unlikely that Carpets were being made here as early as this and it would seem to indicate that cloth had been produced in the Listley Street area in reasonable quantities before this time.

Of the latter that is Tainter Wall, we read "this is on the south side of the lower part of Listley Street, opposite to Messrs. MacMichael's Carpet Factory." From Dr. Pitchford's explanatory notes it would appear that this factory moved to Hospital Street about 1819 as St. Leonard's Schools opened in 1820, probably at first on the premises of the late factory.

In this connection it has now been ascertained that the original school buildings were vested in the National Society as Trustees by various deeds, the first being dated 1st January, 1821, but no plans are available. The property was purchased from Benjamin Bangham who acquired it under a Deed of 25th March, 1818, from the Assignees under the Commission of Bankruptcy.

The buildings are described as "All that carpet factory with the garden and appurtenances thereto belonging situate and being in Bridgnorth aforesaid in a certain Street there called Listley Street on the site of which factory formerly stood three small messuages tenements or dwelling houses."

Associated with the factory at this time were :-

John MacMichael	*Banker*
Thomas Gitton	
William MacMichael	*Banker*
Joseph MacMichael	*Carpet Manufacturer*
Alexander McMath	

The foregoing no doubt explains the reason for the statement in 1824 that "The Carpet trade was a short time ago brought to great perfection here. For a time it was "*discontinued*" but is now going on and is in an increasing state."

At this time William MacMichael had two small factories in the bottom part of Cartway. The one factory would appear to have been nearly opposite to the present "Black Boy" Inn, a building now dismantled and which, within the memory of many of the present generation, was used as a "Soda" factory.

The other, according to Hulbert's History and Description of the County of Salop, 1837, was situated in "the Ancient timber mansion where Dr. Percy, Bishop of Dromore, was born, and who was afterwards proprietor." No deeds are available for this period so that it is uncertain how long carpets were made here, but the premises were later taken over and converted into a Foundry by Samuel Barker. He died in March, 1849, at the age of 41, and as I understand, that he commenced business here on his marriage. It is obvious that carpets ceased to be made in these premises some years previously.

The above was the Grandfather of Samuel Rushton whose family carried on the business until about 1914.

In view of the depressions mentioned earlier in this record it seems well to mention that at this period the trade of the town is said to have been lively, seldom experiencing depression.

The only Carpet Manufacturers mentioned in 1828 are George and William MacMichael & Co.

One can only assume from this that Joseph MacMichael had by this time given up the business and left the district as his name does not appear in any local records. Although this is the only factory mentioned it is known that Southwell & Co., were also in operation at this date.

In 1835, however, we read "The principal manufactory now existing is that for Carpets, carried on by two establishments" but according to a survey map of the Town at that date there were three main Carpet factories apart from many small concerns.

Of the three factories previously mentioned the one in Spital Street, better known as the Pale Meadow Mills, was then in the occupation of Messrs. MacMichael and Grierson, who, in addition to Manufacturing Carpets and Rugs, were also Worsted Spinners and on 1st May, 1838 they acquired the Pendlestone Mills on lease for this latter purpose, for a period of 80 years.

The partners concerned in the transaction were :-

George MacMichael   William MacMichael   Thomas Grierson

but as one of the clauses of the lease permitted them to sublet we find the mills taken over by Thomas Whitmore on 9th June, 1843, for the 75 years still to come. George MacMichael, who had been the London Representative of the firm, was then stated to have previously died.

The Works in Hospital Street were burnt down on 1st July, 1840, but were rebuilt in the same year.

This firm had carpet dealings with Southwell & Co., The Friars, up to 1848, but only Grierson is mentioned in 1849.

In 1851 we find Law and Grierson described as Worsted Spinners, Spital Works, so it would appear that William MacMichael retired from the business between 1848 and 1851 and left the district as again there is no mention of the name in local records.

It is difficult to say when Carpets ceased to be made in these Works as the employees were called together after the Jacquard Power loom had been exhibited and were told about this wonderful loom. This seems to indicate that a Jacquard operated type of carpet was being made.

By 1860 the mill had been taken over by J. B. Grierson, who was described as a Worsted Spinner and no mention is made of Carpets. A possible explanation seems to be that Power Looms were not installed, that the Hand Looms were gradually discarded and Worsted Spinning concentrated upon. He was classified as a Woollen Draper at Waterloo House in 1851, was Mayor of the Borough in 1855 and still an Alderman in 1860. He left the town for Birmingham in August, 1862.

It is peculiar that the Parliamentary Gazetteer 1840-44, in its description of the town does not mention carpets, but stated that "upwards of three fourths of the population are returned as employed in trade and manufactures, the latter being chiefly those of cloth, stockings and iron tools. In 1838 there was a worsted mill here employing 101 hands." It is unlikely that "Cloth" as the term is generally understood, was being made here in any quantity, if at all, at this time and the description probably refers to Carpets, the earliest types of which were flat in character.

However, in Duke's "Antiquities of Shropshire" 1844, we read that "carpeting at Bridgnorth employed from 80 to 90 men" but this figure must be greatly underestimated as a larger number are known to have been employed at "The Friars" about this date.

In 1851 the only Carpet and Rug manufacturers mentioned are :-

Southwell & Co., Friars Road and Pendlestone Mills.

The Carpet factory was at "The Friars" but before this was built the Southwell family are said to have controlled looms in the homes of the workpeople. The history of this factory is described in detail under the title of :-

"The Friars and its Memories" (Part I of this book)

Joseph Southwell, Great Grandfather of Mr. W. Lascelles Southwell, J.P. was the original member of the family to be associated with the Industry. Other members took up the Art, living in various parts of the town.

There is no actual record, but it is practically certain that the factory, built on the present site, adjoining Friars Street, and covering an area of about 5,000 square feet, was commenced between 1824 and 1826, the looms no doubt being then collected into it.

In 1828, however, Southwell & Co. was established by Joseph and William Southwell.

In addition to the above, this Company also had a factory on the "Hand and Bottle" (adjoining Foundry Yard) Estate in April, 1835.

By 1850 this factory had been demolished and several others built and enclosed on ground adjoining the present Malthouse of Wilson and Hood Ltd. Of these Southwells appear to have occupied, at one period, two Factories, Offices and Fitting up rooms but these had been vacated before 5th July, 1855.

Between 1832 and 1840 over 140 were employed in the weaving departments and the works were expanding quickly for before 1850 two two-storey sheds had been built on what are now gardens in front of Coney Villa, in addition to those adjoining Friars Street.

The first types of Carpets produced on the "Hand" looms were those known in the trade as "Kidderminster" followed by various grades of "Venetian" and "Brussels."

With the introduction of "Power" looms the Hand Loom factories were gradually discarded and more suitable sheds built to accommodate these looms.

The first five bays of the main shed were completed by May, 1855, and in this section the first of the new looms were installed in 1858 and used for the manufacture of Brussels Carpet and Rugs.

The firm up to this time had been a family affair, and in addition to the founders of the Company other members assisted in the works in various ways. It was decided, however, to make several changes in the management and eventually in 1860, Mr. Thomas Martin Southwell and Mr. Henry Foxall Southwell, his cousin, took over the factory under the title of H. & M. Southwell, but from 1861 Mr. T. M. Southwell was left in sole control. Some years later, about 1868, further Jacquard looms were added and this enabled a proportion of them to be allotted to the weaving of Wilton Carpets, but a number of Hand Looms were still in production at this date.

In 1879 came the introduction of Power Looms for making the Axminster type of Carpets. This cloth was called Spool Axminster and being much less expensive than the hand made variety soon became very popular, thus necessitating further extensions to the factory.

In 1888 Mr. Southwell took into partnership his three sons, Mr. Horace Southwell, Mr. Edmund Southwell and Mr. William Lascelles Southwell, but in 1890 the firm was floated as a limited Company.

H. & M. SOUTHWELL LTD.

The Axminster department was then increased by the erection of the last five bays of the Main Shed.

Hand knotted Carpets, similar to those originally made at Axminster, were produced during the period 1893-1901. The carpet presented by the Ladies of England to Queen Victoria for the Throne Room on the occasion of her Diamond Jubilee was made here on one of these looms. It contained over 4 1/4 million stitches and took fourteen girls four months to complete.

In 1923 the North Works were commenced on ground adjoining Rope Walk Farm, thus enabling the narrow finishing processes to be carried out more conveniently. Later additional sheds were built and in these the weaving of wide Jacquard and Axminster Carpets were undertaken.

These Works were further extended in 1932 and the firm participated in the making of Tapestry Furnishing Fabrics, but the manufacture of these ceased in 1939. A blanket cloth was woven on a two-needle Axminster loom from the end of 1939 to May, 1941. This cloth was manufactured in two layers, these being joined during weaving at the right hand edge of the loom. The blanket thus produced was double the width of the loom.

The Works today cover an area of about 150,000 square feet. With the retirement of Mr. W. Lascelles Southwell from the Chairmanship of the Company in 1938, the control of "The Friars" passed from the family after more than 100 years.

In addition to the Factories previously occupied by Joseph and William Southwell there were at least two others on the "Bandon Arms" Estate, probably built and owned by Thomas Elcock.

On the 5th July, 1855, he was occupying both the Southwell factories as well as one of the others and was said to be carrying on the Trade or Business of a Carpet Manufacturer.

A further factory was tenanted by Benjamin Saloway.

The Estate also included land used as a Quay or Landing place for the benefit of the Carpet Manufacturers.

At one time Mr. Saloway lived at Cann Hall and had, as a business partner, a Mr. Yates.

Mr. Ben Saloway, son of the above, who lived in St. Mary's Street some 40 years ago, writing from Borden, Saskatchewan, Canada, remembers visiting this factory and seeing the Hand Looms in operation. He also remembers being told that his father had an order from a London firm to make a Royal Carpet and that he was so pleased that, when completed, he put it on show in the Town Hall.

About the time of the introduction of the Power loom, Mr. Yates retired from the Partnership and migrated to Wilton, taking some of the best weavers with him. His father carried on for some time and commenced making Hand tufted carpets, but these were not a financial success and the business was wound up. The dyer was Mr. Lowe, father of Henry Lowe, for many years Head dyer at Southwell's shed, later spoken of as "The Friars."

This building, or a portion of it, was later used for keeping the Rowing Club boats in - but was destroyed by a gale in 1881.

In 1860, Mr. Saloway was making rugs at the then No. 49, Listley Street. He was still described as a rug maker in 1863, so that he must have started further ventures for he is known to have made hand tufted rugs in St. Mary's Street, at the back of No. 57. This building can, no doubt, be remembered as the Blacksmith's shop, run for many years by Mr. Joseph Johnson, from the "Hen and Chickens."

In 1876, the estate included "An old Carpet Manufactory, a garden and ground belonging thereto" so that Carpet Manufacture must have ceased in this area between 1855-1876.

How many smaller factories there were containing only two or three looms is difficult to ascertain.

Mr. John Tyler, father of Mr. James Tyler, is said to have had a hand loom factory in Cartway, opposite to the "Black Boy" Inn - but wisely closed up and joined forces with Southwells when the power loom was introduced.

Mr. Richard Ball, father of Mr. A. W. Ball, designer at Southwells, who is said to have worked at Mr. MacMichael's factory, but is known to have been apprenticed to Joseph Southwell in 1835, had a factory and made rugs in Mill Street, it is believed with the help of a Mr. Wellings. He was assisted as Salesman by John Baker, father of Mrs. Sargeant, of "Coney Villa." In later years he occupied the grocer's shop at the corner of Cartway.

The firm went under the name of Ball & Baker.

Of course it was possible for these small private firms to work any hours, the lighting medium however, was generally candles.

In 1860 only one main factory remained in the town in the Weaving Industry - the Carpet factory of H. & M. Southwell.

It will be seen, therefore, that the first type of carpet to be made in Bridgnorth was doubtless that known in the trade as "Kidderminster." This fabric, flat in character, was formed by the manipulation of Worsted Warps and Woollen Wefts only and could easily have been produced on hand loom; in outbuilding; adjoining the weavers' dwellings, usually being 36 inches in width.

Later when the Jacquard method of selecting the threads or colours for the design came into general use from 1825 onwards, it became necessary to accommodate the looms in larger buildings.

The weaving of Brussels "Looped Pile" and Wilton "Cut Pile" carpets followed in due course.

With the introduction of "Power" looms which followed soon after, their practicability had been shown at the London Exhibition of 1851, the "Hand" looms were gradually discarded and production chiefly concentrated upon the two latter qualities.

Hand tufted carpets in which the pile was knotted to the warp threads and which were developed at Axminster in 1755, were also produced at different periods.

The making of Machine made "Spool" Axminster carpet was commenced in 1879, soon after the looms had been brought over to this country from America and, as mentioned earlier, Bridgnorth has been responsible for many important improvements to these looms since that time.

There is no record of printed Tapestry Carpets having been made here.

Wide Spool Axminster Loom, 1931

CARPET INDUSTRY RESTARTED

The manufacture of carpets having entirely ceased and the machinery dismantled in 1940, doubts possibly arose as to whether carpets would again be made in the town.

In 1943, however, the Directors of the Carpet Manufacturing Co., Kidderminster, became interested in the Works, obtained a controlling interest in the Company, and when a portion of the North Works was released in November, 1944, practically four years after the closing down, the work of replanning the factory and re-erecting the machinery was entrusted to Mr. D. A. Spicer and Mr. F. W. Head.

The first Axminster loom began production in March, 1945, and the re-erection of machinery has gone steadily on despite the difficult conditions of the time.

A prosperous time appears to lie ahead for the employees, as in addition to Axminster and Wilton, the making of Chenille carpets is also being undertaken, a new departure for Bridgnorth. When the necessary machinery has been installed it is expected that production will reach 1,000,000 yards annually, so that although "Time passes on Carpet still remains the staple industry of Bridgnorth."

It is possible that additional information may become available from time to time but the foregoing notes record such facts as have so far been ascertained.

LIST OF WEAVERS AND CARPET WEAVERS
FREEMEN OF BOROUGH

Smith, William	Naughton	Weaver	11 Mar. 1661
Lem, William	Bridgnorth	"	23 Dec. 1674
Broadfield, Thomas	"	"	3 Feb. 1678
Benbow, Thomas	"	"	17 Feb. 1679
Walton, Thomas	Bridgnorth	"	Before 1685
Fields, John	"	"	7 Mar. 1697
Parr, Thomas	Winscott	"	18 April 1698
Morral, Thomas	London	"	13 May 1698
Walton, John	Astley	"	11 May 1702
Preen, William	Kidderminster	"	9 April 1705
Wells, Moses	Bridgnorth	"	6 Oct. 1707
Walton, Benjamin	"	"	26 June 1710
Maiden, William	"	"	26 July 1710
Powell, William	"	"	12 Nov. 1712
Tomkis, Edward	"	"	22 Aug. 1712
Weale, George	"	"	19 Feb. 1721
Leighton, John	"	"	17 April 1721
Bourne, Edward	"	"	7 June 1725
Richards, Walter	"	"	17 July 1727
Stockall, William	Kidderminster	"	17 July 1727
Forsbrooke, Joseph	Bridgnorth	"	14 Aug. 1727
Walton, William	Astley	"	13 Feb. 1732
Cocke, John	App. Moses Welles 1707		13 Feb. 1732
Stockall, Samuel	Bridgnorth	Weaver	6 Aug. 1733
Jewkes, Francis	Coal Green	"	15 Aug. 1733
	App. Wm. Lem 1674		
Malpas, William	Bridgnorth	"	15 July 1739
Guest, William	"	"	28 Jan. 1750
Preen, John	Kidderminster	"	21 June 1756
Jordan, Thomas,	Kidderminster	"	23 April 1759
Son of Richard			
Williams, John	"	Weaver	20 Sept. 1759
Broome, John	Kidderminster	Carpet Weaver	17 July 1769
Guest Edward	"	Weaver	20 Sept. 1771
Wells, William	Worcester	Weaver	13 Jan. 1772
Wells, John	"	"	13 Jan. 1772
Easthope, Edward	Kidderminster	"	7 Mar. 1774
Willis, Thomas	"	"	25 July 1774
Broadfield, Robert	"	"	7 Oct. 1774
Edwards, Joseph	"	"	7 Oct. 1774
Price, Samuel	Bridgnorth	"	7 Oct. 1774
Broadfield, Edward	Kidderminster	"	15 Mar. 1779
Jewkes, Edward	Clee St. Margaret	"	7 April 1784
Edwards, Benjamin		"	9 April 1784
Jordan, William	Bewdley	"	9 April 1784
Son of Samuel	Aston Botterill		
Stockall, Samuel	Kidderminster	"	9 April 1784
James, Thomas	Coventry	"	10 April 1184
James, Thomas, Son of above Coventry		"	10 April 1784
Moseley, John	Kidderminster	"	10 April 1784
Walton, Thomas	Coventry	"	10 April 1784
Price Samuel	Kidderminster	Carpet Weaver	4 June 1786
Andrews, Thomas	Alscot	"	14 Jan. 1788
Price, John	Kidderminster	"	30 May 1796
Jordan, Thomas		"	7 July 1802
Son of Thomas, 1759			

MacMichael, Joseph	Bridgnorth	Carpet Manfr.	21 July 1802
Southwell, Joseph	Bridgnorth	Carpet Weaver	4 Dec. 1809
Broome, John	Kidderminster	Carpet Manfr.	2 July 1810
Broome, Herbert	"	"	2 July 1810
	Sons of John Broome, 17/7/1769		
Walton, Joseph	"	Weaver	21 Sept. 1821
Southwell, Joseph	Bridgnorth	Carpet Weaver	29 Sept. 1824
Southwell, George	"	"	29 Sept. 1824
MacMichael, George	Skinner St. London	Carpet Manfr.	29 Sept. 1825
MacMichael, William	Bridgnorth	"	29 Sept. 1825
Southwell, Thomas Ross	"	Carpet Weaver	29 Sept. 1825
Scott, Gabriel	"	"	16 April 1826
Trevett, Robert	"	"	10 June 1826
Broadfield, Edward	Kidderminster	Weaver	12 June 1826
Broadfield, Robert	"	"	12 June 1826
Jordan, Richard	"	Carpet Weaver	12 June 1826
Percy, George	"	"	12 June 1826
Price, Samuel	"	"	14 June 1826
Minshall, William	Bridgnorth	"	14 June 1826
	App. Joseph Southwell, 1824		
Southwell, Josiah	Kidderminster	Merchants. Clerk	29 Sept. 1826
Hall, William	"	Weaver	11 June 1827
	App. Samuel Price, 7/10/1774		
Stockall, John	Kidderminster	Weaver	21 Sept. 1827
Tolly, John	"	Carpet Weaver	21 Sept. 1827
Danks, Enoch	"	"	21 Sept. 1827
Hayward, Benjamin	"	"	21 Sept. 1827
Southwell, William	Bridgnorth	"	21 Sept. 1827
Southwell, Thomas	"	"	21 Sept. 1827
Crossland, James	"	"	29 Sept. 1827
Jones, William Paul	"	"	29 Sept. 1827
Treadwell, James	"	"	29 Sept. 1827
Bailey, Edward	Bridgnorth	"	29 Sept. 1827
Badland, James	Kidderminster	Weaver	29 Sept. 1827
Pilkington, James	Bridgnorth	"	29 Sept. 1827
Hall, John	"	Carpet Weaver	16 April 1828
Baker, Joseph	Bridgnorth	"	6 June 1828
Barker, James	Bridgnorth	"	6 June 1828
Southwell, George	"	"	29 Sept. 1828
Whitehouse, Thomas	"	"	21 Sept. 1829
Southwell, Thomas	Bridgnorth	"	21 Sept. 1829
Gower, James	| Sons of Wm. Gower	Weaver	26 July 1830
Gower, Thomas	| 1802	"	28 July 1830
Jordan, Benjamin	Kidderminster	Carpet Weaver	28 July 1830
Jordan, John	"	"	3 Aug. 1830
Andrews, Thomas	"	"	3 Aug. 1830
Andrews, Isaac Browne	"	Weaver	4 Aug. 1830
Smith, James	Bridgnorth	Carpet Weaver	7 Jan. 1831
Brown, John	"	"	9 July 1832
Trevett, Aaron	"	"	9 July 1832
Preen, John	App. in Bridgnorth	Carpet Weaver	23 July 1832
Shipman, John	App. in Bridgnorth	"	31 July 1832
Price, Sidney Downes	Bridgnorth	"	29 Dec. 1834
Lloyd, William	"	"	26 Jan. 1835
Ball, Richard	App. Joseph Southwell 1809	"	30 Jan. 1835
Crowther, William	App. Wm. Southwell 1827	"	30 Jan. 1835

Horton, Solomon	App. Joseph Southwell 1824	"	30 Jan. 1835
Lee, Richard	App. Thomas Ross Southwell 1825	"	30 Jan. 1835
Southwell, John	App. to George and William MacMichael	Writing Clerk	30 Jan. 1835
Moseley, John		Carpet Weaver	13 July 1835
Page, Frances		"	13 July 1835
Lloyd, Edward		"	20 July 1835
Goodwin, John Ambrose		"	27 July 1835
Baker, William	Bridgnorth App. Joseph Baker, 6/6/1828	"	26 July 1838
Longmore, Henry	App. to Wm. Hall and Thomas Ross Southwell	"	26 July 1838
Meads, John	App. Edward Bailey 29/9/1827	"	30 July 1841
Southwell, Henry Foxall	App. Josiah Southwell 29/9/1826	"	10 Feb. 1843
Tolley, William	App. John Tolley 21/8/1827	"	2 Feb. 1844
Beech, Edwin	App. Joseph and Wm. Southwell	"	9 Feb. 1846
Tyler, Samuel			9 Feb. 1846
Southwell, Benjamin	App. George Southwell 29/9/1828	"	23 July 1847
Head, Thomas, Son of Edward the Tailor		"	23 July 1847
Head, Edwin		"	23 July 1847
Brown, Charles	Bridgnorth	Carpet Weaver	23 July 1847
Jones, John	Bridgnorth App. Joseph Southwell, 29/9/1824	"	23 July 1847
Baker, Benjamin	App. Joseph Baker 6/6/1828	"	15 Aug. 1849
Evans, James	Bridgnorth	Weaver	26 July 1850
Evans, Joseph	"	"	26 July 1850
Southwell, William	Cartway, Bridgnorth App. George Southwell, 29/9/1828	"	7 Jan. 1851
Southwell, Joseph	Friars St. Bridgnorth App. Thomas Southwell, 21/9/1829	Carpet Weaver	13 July 1852
Caust, William	Cartway, Bridgnorth App. Thomas Southwell, 21/9/1829	Carpet Weaver	30 July 1852
Jordan, Frederick		Carpet Weaver	25 July 1862
Jordan, John		"	29 July 1865
Head, John	| Sons of Edwin	"	Aug. 1872
Head, Thomas William	| Carpet Weaver	Foreman Carpet Works	21 Dec. 1901
Southwell, William Lascelles, J.P. (Honorary)			9 Oct. 1935

   Chairman of H. & M. Southwell Ltd. Carpet Works.

Part III - The Post War Boom Years

WARTIME IN THE CARPET INDUSTRY

The fortunes of the carpet industry suffered in many ways during the Second World War. At the start, the Board of Trade pronounced that carpets were "non-essential goods" and, nationally, fourteen "nucleus" carpet companies were licensed to manufacture a limited production for as long as the raw materials remained available. Strict controls made sure that the carpet produced was connected with the war effort. Export orders were encouraged, but retail production was totally stopped.

With so much production space and so many looms the Kidderminster companies were able to consider a variety of options. The carpet loom had the capability of weaving fabrics and so, a number of Axminster and Wilton looms were set up to weave materials such as blankets and the webbing for haversacks. Other looms were dismantled and put into store, thus creating space for machinery for the production of small arms and ammunition, all under the control of the Ministry of Supply. Surplus buildings and factory space became stores. On the shop floor new skills were needed and it became difficult to balance these skills as the young men and women left to join the armed forces.

Several of the larger Kidderminster companies were given "nucleus" status. However, H.&M.Southwell of Bridgnorth was not included and so, as their raw materials became reduced, they had to rely more and more on the Kidderminster "nucleus" companies to weave the carpet for their outstanding orders. Therefore, they restricted their carpet production and looked for other possibilities for their Axminster and Wilton looms.

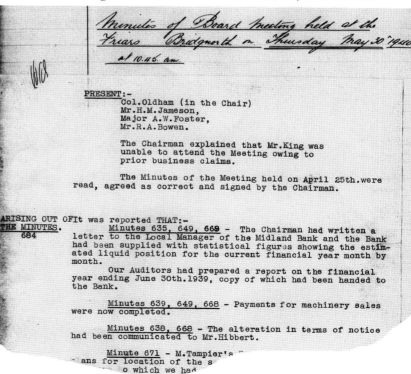

H. & M. SOUTHWELL LTD.
- THE BOARD MINUTES TELL THE STORY

The Board Minute Book No.6 is a large green ledger that recorded the operations of the company during the Second World War. Starting in January 1940, the typed minutes outline the decisions made by the board of directors. The Chairman was Col. H.L.Oldham and the other members were H.M.Jameson, Major.A.W.Foster, H.S.King and R.A.Bowen.
The following is a précis of this historical record now in the keeping of The Carpet Museum Trust :

The period between the two World Wars had been a time for consolidation and recovery within the carpet industry. Although the Southwell company was financially stable it had not made a profit for some years and the Midland Bank was cautious about the future. Therefore they requested the directors to take actions to reduce the overdraft. After due consideration, they took the unusual step of selling off some of their equipment to their competitors. Bond Worth, of Stourport, bought four Wilton Jacquard looms; Morris Carpets of Kidderminster bought six Spool Axminster looms and more looms were purchased for a carpet factory in Ontario, Canada. Other saleable items, such as dye-vats, were sold in order to make ends meet. Although their outgoings were minimal, they did have some expenditure; for example, it became necessary to buy a seven-hundredweight van for £173 !

In the factory they were experimenting with the conversion of looms to weave war products. Early samples of "Nitidax" blankets were encouraging and these were attracting interest from potential customers. The Gaumont-British Picture Corporation expressed concerns about the outstanding part of their order for cinema carpeting. However, the raw materials were strictly rationed and in short supply and so the Board were forced to consider other possibilities. Unrationed fibres such as horsehair, Fibro and yarns made from Kraft paper were examined in detail, but they were not really suitable for heavy-duty carpet installations.

The Board members were not backward in their planning for the future and so, when coal supplies for the boilers were under threat, they released money to stockpile during the summer months. By June 1940 trade was rapidly declining due to the collapse of France. The position was made worse when the Government introduced a new "Restriction of Purchases" order. However, the sale of Nitidax blankets was still buoyant and in July, with all these factors in mind, they took the decision to concentrate what was left of their weaving production in North Works.

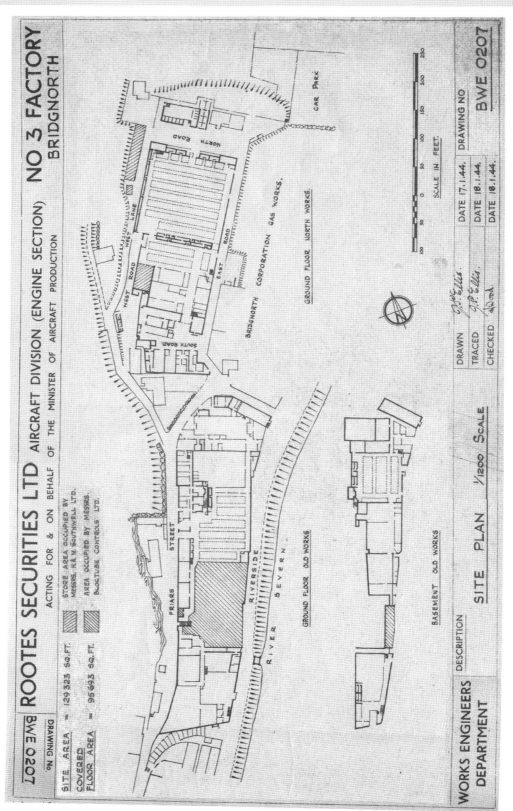

ROOTES SECURITIES LTD AIRCRAFT DIVISION (ENGINE SECTION)
NO 3 FACTORY
BRIDGNORTH

ACTING FOR & ON BEHALF OF THE MINISTER OF AIRCRAFT PRODUCTION

DRAWING NO BWE 0207

SITE AREA = 129 323 SQ.FT.
COVERED
FLOOR AREA = 95 693 SQ.FT.

STORE AREA OCCUPIED BY
MESSRS. H.& M. SOUTHWELL LTD.

AREA OCCUPIED BY MESSRS.
BLACKTUBE CONTROLS LTD.

SCALE IN FEET.

GROUND FLOOR NORTH WORKS.

BRIDGNORTH CORPORATION GAS WORKS.

CAR PARK

NORTH ROAD

EAST ROAD

SOUTH ROAD

WEST ROAD

WEST LANE

FRIARS STREET

RIVERSIDE

RIVER SEVERN

GROUND FLOOR OLD WORKS

BASEMENT OLD WORKS

WORKS ENGINEERS
DEPARTMENT

DESCRIPTION
SITE PLAN   1/1200 SCALE

DRAWN   G.P. Ellis.   DATE 17.1.44.
TRACED G.P. Ellis.   DATE 18.1.44.
CHECKED W.B.   DATE 18.1.44.

DRAWING NO
BWE 0207

But the writing was on the wall and the minutes of October 1940 record the visit in September to Friars Works by officials from the Ministry of Supply who were accompanied by representatives from Rootes Securities of Coventry. They toured the whole site considering the possibilities of converting floor space to the production of important aircraft engine parts. As a direct result, H. & M. Southwell were served with immediate requisitioning papers that instructed the company to release all its production space to Rootes. Contracts were quickly drawn up to include rent and the conditions of return once the war was over. During the following months the name of Thomas Ward & Son was added to the contract.

And so weaving in Bridgnorth came to a temporary halt. Fred Head recorded the sad details in his diary, "I wove the last piece of 4/4 (yard wide) waste runner on E.Preece's loom at 4.45pm on 4th October 1940. A.James wove the last Atkinson Rug on 4th November and the last piece of Wilton, in 4/5814 Brown Chester quality, was woven by R.Baker on 12th November 1940. Cleared my office 14th November 1940." For the remaining war years Fred Head worked for Rootes Securities where he was able to keep an eye on the carpet machinery in store.

Arrangements were immediately made for W.&R.R.Adam of Kidderminster, a "nucleus" company, to weave Southwell's outstanding carpet orders, and the necessary redundancy notices were prepared for the few remaining shop-floor employees. In the early part of 1941 The Chlidema Carpet Company and Woodward Grosvenor, both of Kidderminster, were also weaving Southwell orders but with difficulty, due to problems in the supply of jute. Up until this time the company administered its affairs from the registered office in South Works where it also retained a showroom and a small warehouse. In June, however, under pressure from the Ministry of Supply, the Board approved plans to move lock, stock and barrel from South Works to premises known as "The Old Castle Brewery." On a lesser issue the Board also gave permission for one of its remaining employees to devote mornings to his duties with the local Home Guard Battalion, although his wages would be reduced by £2 per week.

By 1942 Board Meetings were being held in London at 201 Great Portland Place. In April the Chairman, Col.H.L.Oldham, presented plans for the complete termination of trading. Disposal of the stock of raw material, woven carpet and the remaining staff was the big issue, but they also reviewed their own board positions. There seemed to be a major problem in storing the dismantled machinery and equipment which was still scattered around Friars Works. One of the options on offer was to transfer to a competitor in Kidderminster. During these troubled times the company tried to remain viable and so the Board discussed the possibility of setting up a munitions manufacturing company of their own.

In December 1942 the Carpet Export Group Executive Committee was instructed by the Board of Trade that "all carpet manufacture should cease on 30th November 1942." Subsequently, the remaining yarn was sold and the company was instructed to remove its machinery from Friars Works forthwith. However, after some discussion, a concession was agreed and some selected machinery was stored in North Works. Under the terms of the Company Constitution the company was not allowed to form a munitions company using the Southwell name, but it was suggested, that it could set up a separate company using the name "The Bridgnorth Engineering Company." From 1st January 1943 D.A.Spicer was appointed to organise and supervise the transfer of the remaining plant and machinery to Brinton's factory in Kidderminster.

The May 1943 Board Meeting was well attended, the Chairman reporting that he had received three offers to purchase the Southwell company; two from competitors and one via the Anglo-Federal Banking Corporation. By July, after many independent meetings and discussions, it was apparent that The Carpet Manufacturing Company of Kidderminster was the forerunner and that detail meetings were taking place. By the end of July agreements had been struck and three of their directors had been appointed to the Southwell Board.

Col. Oldham summed up the situation in a statement to the board when he declared that he hoped the "new association would be of benefit to both companies and to the town of Bridgnorth." Col.Oldham then resigned and The Carpet Manufacturing Company's E.H.O.Carpenter was appointed the new Chairman.

At this point the green Board Minute Book of H. & M. Southwell became history and was committed to the company safe. In the 1990s, following the demise of Coloroll, it was recovered from a skip and is now part of the Archive Collection belonging to The Carpet Museum Trust.

H. & M. Southwell, Ltd.,
Bridgnorth.

Telegrams—Southwell, Bridgnorth.   Telephone No. 12 Bridgnorth.

Letter headings :- Note Southwell's telephone number!

TELEPHONE:
2271.

BY APPOINTMENT

TO H.M. THE KING

TELEGRAMS
CARMANCO.

THE CARPET MANUFACTURING Co. LTD.
MORTON & SONS ASSOCIATING RICHARD SMITH & SONS
H. & M. SOUTHWELL LTD.. BRIDGNORTH.

KIDDERMINSTER.

THE CARPET MANUFACTURING COMPANY (CMC)

The Carpet Manufacturing Company was formed in 1890 when Richard Smith & Sons of Mill Street combined with James Morton & Sons of New Road to form a large manufacturing company with a number of locations in and around Kidderminster. The reason they combined forces was due to the efforts of an accountant called Harvey Preen who had been in negotiations with all the notable carpet manufacturers with the aim of forming one large company under the title "The Carpet Alliance." It is ironical that the Southwell Company was one of those originally targeted for membership of this alliance. Further, had the deal gone through, it had been agreed that Thomas Martin Southwell would have been the first Managing Director. However, this was not to be and the proposal failed except for the two above-mentioned firms, which formed themselves into, what was at the time, the largest carpet company in Kidderminster.

H. & M. SOUTHWELL REFORMED

The Carpet Manufacturing Company was now firmly in control and immediately set up plans to get the factory weaving again once the War had ended and the restrictions removed. In Kidderminster it owned a number of sites around the town and it was not unusual to see its dark green vans and lorries transporting raw materials and finished carpets from one site to another. The Bridgnorth factory became another of these satellite locations, though it lay 15 miles north of Kidderminster.

In hindsight, the take-over was good for the Southwell company because it would have had great difficulty in financing its own return to production. With the industry in revival, production machinery, both new and second-hand, was expensive and hard to come by and it would have been virtually impossible to reform H.&M.Southwell as a self-contained operation. With the backing of CMC the future was assured.

Plans were agreed that the Friars Works would become a predominantly weaving establishment. Materials in the form of dyed yarns and other raw materials would be brought to Bridgnorth for conversion into carpet. After weaving, the carpet would be returned to Kidderminster for finishing, warehousing and distribution. In those days the operations surrounding the weaving process were very labour intensive and so local employment was guaranteed. Thus, North Works was laid out to receive Spool Axminster together with a small Wilton plant and South Works designed to house Chenille Axminster weaving. Fred Head, now re-employed by CMC, and D.A.Spicer were given the task of co-ordinating this return to production. The first yard of Spool Axminster carpet was woven in March 1945.

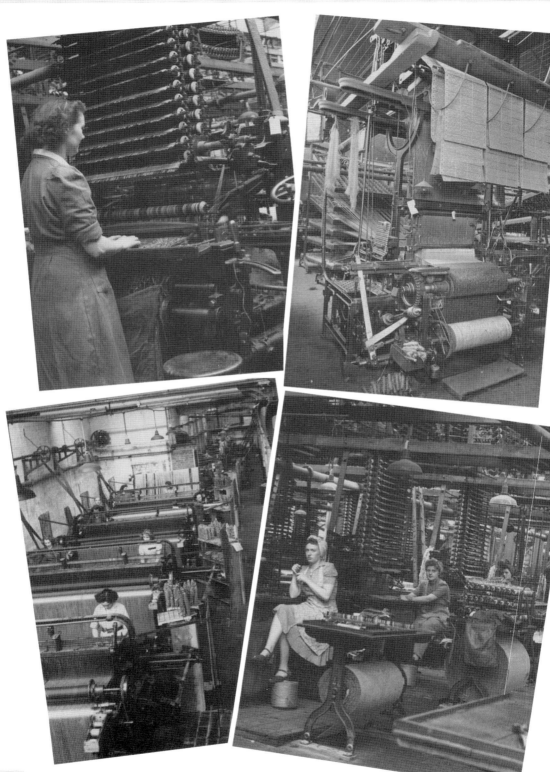

THE BOOM YEARS OF THE 1950s

With the Government manufacturing restrictions removed and the supply of raw materials assured, the carpet manufacturers returned to productivity with a vengeance. The world had been starved of British woven carpet and the export markets opened up. The Government-sponsored house-building programme created new estates, all wanting "wall-to-wall" carpet. The old square on top of "lino" was outdated. And so, with full order books, it was boom time for the carpet industry. During the years to follow some of CMC's most popular qualities were woven at the Friars Works. These included "Globe" Spool Axminster and the hardwearing "Debrett" Jacquard Wilton.

In the early years following the war A.G.(Tony) Roden was the General Manager and he lived at "Friars House" which had been known locally as "Coney Villa." The house was built on the hillside overlooking Friars Street and the South Works. Times were good and the company spirit prevailed. The range of skills in the carpet industry provided employment for whole families, many had originally worked for the Southwells. The company was well represented in the local sports leagues and the works canteen, together the Friars Social Club with George Ward in control,

became the location for many a party. The *Bridgnorth Journal* reported these events in detail. Typical was the New Year's Party in 1951 when Ted Price & his Band played for 300 partygoers. Entertainment consisted of songs by Rosa Perks and Albert Webb; N.Bromage, comedian; Cardovani, magician and Miss Brenda Camben and the Della School of Dance.

In 1951 it was sad to report the deaths of two former directors who were both Freemen of the Borough of Bridgnorth. In January, Thomas William Head, JP, died aged 86. He had worked for H.&M.Southwell from 1874 until his retirement in 1929. In the carpet industry, he will be best remembered for his improvements to the Spool Axminster Loom. The Rev. Wallace Cox conducted the funeral service at St.Leonard's Church. In March, William Lascelles Southwell died at his home in Llandrindod Wells, aged 96. He was a prominent Conservative and Freemason. CMC was represented at the funeral by directors E.H.O.Carpenter and W.P.W. (Peter) Anderson.

In June 1951, E.H.O.Carpenter presented ten employees with gold watches in recognition of more than 50 years service to the company. Charles Jordan was proud of his 64 years !

By now, Thomas William Head's son, Fred, had responsibilities and an office in Kidderminster, but his first love was the Friars factory where he would call every morning to make sure things were going according to plan. His interest in the

history of Bridgnorth's carpet industry was still very much alive and in June 1951 he put on an Exhibition in the Burgess' Hall, Northgate.

It is interesting to note that the Northgate itself was renovated in 1910 by public subscription in memory of Thomas Martin Southwell who was known as "The Grand Old Man of Bridgnorth."

Note : Today, the Burgess' Hall is the home of The Northgate Museum. One of the exhibits is an old wooden handloom originally belonging to the Southwell company. Dating back to the early 1800s it is typical of the looms used in the cottage industry of the town.

It is a well recorded fact that the Industrial Revolution started for the carpet industry at Queen Victoria's Great Exhibition in 1851 where the American, Erastus Bigelow, exhibited the first carpet power-loom. One hundred years later, in 1951, the country was celebrating "The Festival of Britain" and Bridgnorth had its organising committee. One of the attractions on offer was a 45-minute tour around the Friars Street factory to see the weaving looms. However, the one part of the factory that was out of bounds was under the arches in the basement of South Works on the river side, for it was there that "Old Mo" was known to make occasional appearances.

"Old Mo" was the ghost of a Franciscan Monk who chose odd moments to appear as he did to workmen in December 1951. Just above, in the Picking Room, was the location of the Annual Children's Christmas Party where 120 children of employees gathered for tea and games. Local character George

"Evergreen" Gower (below, sitting on the floor) led the songs before a fairy, Miss

Helen Briggs, whose father, Terry, was the Company Secretary, stepped out of a Christmas Card and waved her wand to signal the entry of a sledge full of gifts for the children.

Fortunately, "Old Mo" gave this party a miss !

Peter Anderson was the guest speaker at Southwell's Fire Service Dinner in December 1952. He paid tribute to the Works Fire Brigade and particularly their Chief Officer J.A.(Bert) James (extreme left-hand side of the 1940 photograph).

These Annual Dinners seemed to be a platform for reviewing the company fortunes and, that year, he went on to predict a good future for the industry, CMC and its Bridgnorth operation.

Friars Works continued to produce some fine woven carpets. In 1952 two very special carpets were woven in best quality Axminster following an order from the Rhodes Centenary Committee in South Africa. The first depicted Victoria Falls and the features of "Cecil Rhodes, Empire Builder 1853-1953." The second was a beautiful design with pink elephants in wine glasses on a green background. Hard wearing Wilton was popular in the licensing trade, one loom was permanently set up to weave rugs for the breweries including Ansells, Threlfalls and M&B.

1953 - AS REPORTED BY Bridgnorth Journal

and South Shropshire Advertiser

No. 5,049. Registered at the General Post Office as a Newspaper. FRIDAY, APRIL 6, 1951. Postal Subscription: 6/6 per half-year; 13/- per year PRICE 2d

While the carpet works were thriving, the town of Bridgnorth was having its ups and downs. St.Leonard's Church tower was in need of repair and had launched an appeal for £20,000. One of their bell ringers, Horace William Overton, had just completed 63 years service at Southwells, having started at the age of twelve. The NEW Austin Seven was on sale at Bridgnorth Garage in West Castle Street.

A British Rail ticket to Kidderminster would set you back 2/3d and Foxall's Tours ran a weekly coach service to Blackpool. In March, at the Majestic Cinema, you could

FOXALL and SONS
COACH TOURS

SALOON COACHES will leave POSTERN GATE on
To-morrow—Saturday, April 7
GRAND NATIONAL RACE AT LIVERPOOL at   a.m.
Monday, April 9
QUATFORD WHIST DRIVE at 7 p.m.
CLAVERLEY WHIST DRIVE at 7 p.m.
Thursday, April 12
MORVILLE MILITARY WHIST DRIVE at 7 p.m.
Friday, April 13
WORFIELD DANCE at 8.15 p.m.
ALVELEY WHIST DRIVE at 7.15 p.m.
Further particulars and bookings apply :
38 Underhill Street, Bridgnorth. TEL. 2192

MAJESTIC ABC
BRIDGNORTH (Phone: 3274)
FREE CAR PARK AVAILABLE FOR PATRONS ONLY   ARDENTE DEAF AIDS FOR THE DEAF
Sunday next—Humphrey Bogart, Lizabeth Scott DEAD RECKONING A
Gloria Henry, Ross Ford AIR HOSTESS U

Monday, April 9 — for 3 days
Sterling HAYDEN   Louis CALHERN   Hedy LAMARR   John HODIAK in
Jean HAGEN in
The Asphalt Jungle   **A LADY WITHOUT PASSPORT**
at 1.45, 5.00, 8.15   A   at 3.25, 6.45   A

Thursday, April 12 for 3 days   at 2.40, 5.35, 8.30
Margaret JOHNSTON   Richard TODD   Robin BAILEY
Portrait of Claire U
LON McCALLISTER   LOIS BUTLER
BLAZE OF GLORY U
at 4.10, 7.05
A.B.C. FILM REVIEW—April Issue—Now on Sale, Price 4d.

have settled down to see Monkey Business with Marilyn Monroe and Cary Grant. In the Council Chamber much debate was caused by an increase in the Borough rate, which went up by 1/6d in the £1. However, this was not as much as the rumpus caused by Alderman J.W.C.Bowers when he demanded to know from the Town Coronation Celebrations Committee - "Who is going to pay for the roasting ox ?"

MORE ABOUT THE 1950s

Factory life was good and there was much to do. Fred Head's brother, George, was in charge of the Axminster production and Ernest Delo was the Union shop secretary. Roy Westcott ran Chenille. George Smallman was the Chief Engineer in charge of a small well-equipped workshop. In the office, Miss Askew and Miss Dorothy Christian ruled the roost. The canteen was a popular meeting and eating-place for all occasions including the visit of the live radio lunchtime programme Workers Playtime, which featured the singing stars of the day, Pearl Carr and Teddy Johnson. Manageress, Vi Perry, produced the goods! Company transport was kept in order by Edgar Crockson and Sister Lawton's surgery was clean and tidy. Good sports facilities existed on the fields along the riverside and the company owned the fishing rights.

Although carpet sales were generally good, there were odd times when the company had to introduce short time for some of its qualities. The main concern was the declining markets for Chenille Axminster and Jacquard Wilton. In June 1955 the *Journal* carried the headline "First Big Effect of the Rail Strike" as 400 carpet workers were reduced to a three-day week.

In the latter part of the decade the *Journal* carried photographs of the new buildings at the Star Aluminium factory. In May 1957 Princess Marina, the Duchess of Kent, unveiled the Memorial Gates to the Castle Grounds and she also visited an exhibition in the Town Hall where the Southwell company had put on a display entitled "60 Years of Carpet Weaving at the Friars Factory." The Duchess was particularly intrigued by a small sample of the hand-knotted carpet that had been presented to Queen Victoria in 1897.

Note : In Part.1 of this book Fred Head gives the details of the beautiful hand-knotted carpet presented to Queen Victoria in 1897. Three of the ladies who worked on the carpet were Nelly, Annie and their mother Mrs R.Shergold. In the late 1970s another sister Nina, now Mrs Evans and in her 80s, received a copy of a letter from the Master of the Household at Windsor Castle addressed to her brother Hubert Shergold. The letter confirmed that the carpet was still laid in one of the State Rooms on the ground floor at Buckingham Palace. In 2003 the author of this section also wrote to Buckingham Palace on behalf of The Carpet Museum Trust. This time the reply came from The Royal Collection Trust who confirmed that the Southwell Jubilee Carpet was still in good order and laid in "The 1855 Room" at the Palace. Unfortunately the room is in the private area and cannot be viewed. Could it be that the Royal Corgies enjoy the lush pile ?

In September 1957 Bridgnorth was the location for CMC's Annual Sales Conference where, for two days, Geoffrey Allen, the Sales Director, addressed the sales team and introduced the new product ranges. In October, it was literally all hands to the pump as the workforce fought off the worst flooding for ten years when the River Severn burst its banks. In the early years the Southwell company owned many of the small cottages in Friars Street. Southwell employees rented the cottages where, originally, cloth would have been woven on handlooms in the upper rooms. After the war ownership was transferred to CMC and, around this time, they sold the cottages to the existing tenants for the princely sum of £35 !

THE SWINGING SIXTIES AND NEW TECHNOLOGY

The boom in carpet sales continued into the 1960s and, like most companies, CMC were active in the contract market. Hotels, casinos and cruise ships provided big business.

Man-made fibres were being introduced and for the first time blends of nylon and wool combined to improve the wear properties of the pile surface. On the domestic front, Globe quality continued to sell well and CMC had a winner with the "Skaters Trail" design, which sold over a

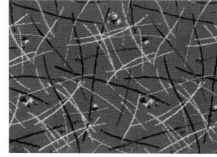

Now...
GLOBE **Axminster and** **BRI NYLON**
get together – to give you
an even better broadloom with a
longer, lovelier life!

million square yards. However, sales of Chenille Axminster and, to a lesser extent, patterned Wilton were even more in decline.

With good profits in the bank most of the carpet companies were looking at ways to improve their efficiencies and increase production levels. The introduction of "Tufted Carpet" in the mid-1950s was beginning to take off as more weaving companies invested in these more productive machines. The Tufting operation involves reciprocating needles which "podge" tufts into a preformed backing at very high speeds. Although considerably faster than the weaving process, the early products were mainly plain colours and of questionable quality.

CMC's stake in this growing tufting technology came from their investment in Kosset Carpets Ltd. of Brighouse, Yorkshire. In this venture The Carpet Manufacturing Company were equal partners with Brintons, John Crossley-Carpet Trades Holdings and Templetons of Glasgow in the company set up in 1955. T.Bond Worth of Stourport was more cautious and retained a half share.

However, the whole industry was also looking at other ways of making carpet. Flatbed and rotary-screen printing machines, originally designed for cloth, were adapted to print the cheaper tufted carpet. The results were not spectacular but designs were suitable for bedrooms and other low-wear locations. The need for special floor coverings for hospitals, aeroplanes and installations where dust and static electricity was a problem led companies to examine the use of synthetic fibres and plastics. The growth of special computer rooms with a need to access under floor wires created a growth in the market for "Carpet tiles" which could be quickly removed and replaced. Collectively, these developments were known as "non-wovens" because they were not constructed on a loom in the traditional way. CMC knew all about these and their research led them to invest and develop a novel pleated carpet system, which they later christened Debron.

THE BIRTH OF DEBRON

It all started in the early sixties when company directors were invited to look over the French liner *France*. Like all good carpet men they examined the ship's floor coverings and were surprised to find an extremely hardwearing and serviceable non-woven carpet in place. Enquiries led them to the factory of the French inventor Pierre Couquet. Couquet had invented a process that literally folded or "pleated" a sheet of carpet yarns on to a steel bed. The yarns were held in position with a pliable newsprint paper, the paper folding with the yarn. A plastic adhesive was spread and cured to both sides of the pleated yarns and the resulting fabric split through the middle to form two sheets of cutpile carpet. Negotiations between Couquet and CMC were concluded and the licence to manufacture and further develop the product was in place.

In later years *France* was re-registered as *Norway*, and CMC was awarded the contract to carpet the ship.

The decline and removal of the Chenille Axminster plant in South Works provided much needed space for expansion. The narrow Jacquard Wilton looms were transferred from North Works giving the opportunity to extend Axminster. However, part of South Works was screened off for the new non-woven development. Geoffrey Head (no relation to Fred Head) was asked to lead a small development team consisting of Roy Herring, Graham Scott and Sid Butler. The team visited Couquet's factory and recalled the "Heath-Robinson" design of his equipment, but the concept was sound and it led to the construction of the first "pleating" machine for Bridgnorth. It was a monster and was instantly christened "Big Bertha" (photograph page 68). However, it proved a point and subsequent production machines were smaller and more accessible. In the early years the process was top-secret and those involved were sworn to secrecy, visitors were required to sign a secrecy form for which they were paid £1 !

The name Debron was chosen because of its likeness to the extremely hardwearing Wilton Debrett quality. After a suitable development and evaluation period the company was ready to market the carpet at 54ins width. In 1964 Debron Carpets Ltd. was

registered with Story Brothers of Lancaster as a one-third partner. Storeys provided the expertise for the backing plastic adhesives.

Some of the first production was tested locally in a High Street shoe shop. But these early products produced some challenges. The finished rolls of carpet were heavy due to the weight of the PVC backing and this led to problems. One of these involved the fact that some plastics became brittle in extremely cold conditions. The story is told that a roll of Debron was sent to Canada during the winter when the temperature was well below freezing. Unfortunately, during unloading, the heavy bale slipped out of its sling and fell on the dockside causing a number of cracks in the backing. The story became a good talking point around the factory and so designer Stanley Colburn produced a cartoon to record the event for posterity.

These problems were soon overcome however and eventually the introduction of a fibreglass mesh into the PVC backing gave the carpet its stability on the floor. At the Mayfair Hotel in London Jim Carpenter pronounced, "with its 100% Bri-Nylon pile, bonded into a PVC backing held firm with fibreglass it is, perhaps, the toughest carpet ever produced." Further development concentrated on the contract tile market and in 1968 Barclay's Bank took delivery of the first tile installation.

1969 WAS A "MILESTONE" YEAR

In 1969 the company was still very buoyant and there was good employment for the 350 workforce at the Bridgnorth factory. Scotsman David Taylor was the Works Manager of the weaving operation and he now lived in Friars House. He proved to be a popular figure in High Street as he led the weekly "wages team" to the bank. The team consisted of Miss Christian and two "heavies" selected from the workforce !

By this time Debron was well established with Derek Westwood selling the products and Sid Moule running the production. While

Debron was self-contained in Bridgnorth the weaving operation still relied on the fleet of lorries pounding the road between Bridgnorth and Kidderminster.

However, the big event of 1969 was the merger of The Carpet Manufacturing Company with its competitor John Crossley-Carpet Trades Holdings to form the largest carpet manufacturing group in Europe and they called themselves Carpets

International Ltd. CIL was large. As well as the Kidderminster-based companies they owned factories in Yorkshire and a number of countries abroad. The Yorkshire companies included Kosset Carpets and the Illingworth Felt Company at Shelf, near Halifax, where they also made carpet tiles. Debron Carpets, being part of CMC, now became one of the Carpet International Companies.

THE SHAKY SEVENTIES

The boom years of the 1950s and 60s were now at an end. Worldwide, over investment in the carpet industry had resulted in overproduction. Uncontrolled foreign imports flooded into this country. Many of the UK carpet companies had also overstepped the mark and were having to tighten their belts. Carpets International was no exception and in 1971 they restructured the operation and formed a Northern and a Southern Division, the latter including the Bridgnorth factory.

In 1972 David Taylor retired after 34 years with the company. He had been associated with Bridgnorth since 1950. The workforce continued to play its part in the life of the town. The CMC teams still competed in local sport and in 1973 the Bridgnorth Amateur Operatic Society staged Gilbert & Sullivan's Iolanthe. Two of Debron's stalwarts played their part; Alf Rudd was the producer and Doug Baker starred as Private Willis. In Bridgnorth, there was full employment and school leavers had a good choice of jobs. CMC were advertising for setters and winders

but the local 18-year-old young ladies could earn £16 a week at Star Aluminium or assembling colour televisions at Decca's Pale Meadow Mill. It had been some years since MacMichael's carpet factory had occupied Decca's Hospital Street site. For newly-married couples a new "semi" on Lodge Farm would set you back £8,150!

Debron continued to be a winner. The PVC backing made the 54-inch-wide sheet material easy to join in a way that was virtually invisible. However, the real growth was in the tile market and, as sales grew, so the plant expanded taking up more of South Works. This meant that the Wilton Jacquard looms had to be

relocated to Kidderminster. However, this expansion did have a downside because of the fumes emanating from the PVC during the heat-curing process. Local residents complained and so the company installed filter equipment to eliminate the smells.

In the early years of Debron an American called Ray Anderson visited the company. At that time he worked for a large American tile manufacturer. In the early 1970s he returned with a proposition that he put to Carpets International for a new company in LaGrange, Georgia. After a period of evaluation Carpets International (Georgia) Inc. was launched in 1972. CIGI, as it became affectionately known, concentrated solely on the tile market with the Debron tile as one of its products. New equipment was produced locally at Olivers Engineering Company. These were exciting times as Debron's Sid Butler together with Melvyn Thompson (the author) were dispatched to LaGrange in Georgia to set up the first batch of production equipment. CIGI grew rapidly and eventually changed its name to Interface Flooring Systems. In a strange twist of fortunes Interface were, in later years, to have a significant influence on the fate of Debron in Bridgnorth.

Part IV - The End of an Era

1975 WAS NOT A GOOD YEAR !

The Nationwide recession in most industries was now taking hold. The country was gripped by events surrounding the missing heiress Lesley Whittle; Star Aluminium was announcing some redundancies at all their factories; Decca was planning a four-day week and the closure of St.Leonard's Church seemed inevitable. But the big headline in the March 27th copy of the *Journal* pronounced "Carpet Factory to move its Axminster Department out of Bridgnorth." The Southern Division of Carpets International was cutting costs and the 15 miles of roadway between Kidderminster and Bridgnorth was a major consideration. It was no consolation to the workforce in Bridgnorth to know that CIL was also closing their satellite factories in Kidderminster with the loss of many jobs. However, the only item of good news for Bridgnorth was that Debron production was to remain in South Works. By this time they had established a warehouse in the riverside shed in North Works making Debron production completely independent of Kidderminster.

Spool Axminster in Bridgnorth employed a workforce of around 200 and some of those affected were offered a transfer with their looms. Initially 50 took up the offer. The Mill Street site in Kidderminster was reorganised to accept the broad Spool Axminster looms into one shed that was instantly christened "The Bridgnorth Shed." With a desire to keep production moving the relocation timescale was extended and it was not until 1977 that the last Axminster loom left the Friars factory.

Since Debron was a non-woven product it could be argued that 1977 was the year that "weaving" ceased in Bridgnorth.

LIFE GOES ON

In June 1975 they had a children's party in the canteen. Once again George "Evergreen" Gower was in control despite his 92 years. The press reported that George had been a chorister for 87 years, 60 of those in St.Leonard's. In the following month the company pensioners went to Stratford-on-Avon for the day. They ended up at the CMC Social Club in Green Street Kidderminster for a buffet and a "knees-up."

However, Friars Works was not the only carpet factory in the area. Chanter Carpets was the name of a carpet company in Alveley which was established in 1971. Contrary to the trend, in the mid-1970s, they were expanding and had applied to Bridgnorth District Council for permission to build an extension. Although they were basically Axminster weavers they did invest in a more productive Tufter that was delivered in January 1976. In the same month "100 get the chop at Decca" ran the headline as the introduction of VAT was blamed for a downturn in orders. Peter Anderson, who lived at Yonder Wyken, Worfield, retired as Chief Executive of Carpets International and later that year Sid Moule and Derek Westwood shared in the success of Debron Ltd. when they were appointed Directors of the company.

In 1978 Decca commenced a short stay in the former weaving sheds of North Works and the skyline changed as steeplejacks demolished Southwell's old 115-foot-high square boilerhouse chimney in Friars Street. Chanter Carpets were taken over by Queensway Securities which immediately announced "No redundancies", but the writing was on the wall and a year later 40 of their workforce were "working to rule" in a dispute over pay. By November the company had failed and was in receivership. Cakebole Carpets ran the business until 1981 when a group of Middle Eastern businessmen took over. They later ceased trading and the company closed.

THINGS GET WORSE IN THE 1980s

The general decline in British industry was reflected at Decca as Racal Electronics took over and then sold out to Tatung. In the carpet industry imports, particularly from America, were flooding into this country uncontrolled by the European Common Market. However, Debron, with Roy Delo in control of 65 employees, seemed to be thriving as the company announced an "Autumn Upsurge" in August 1981. Around this time the popular radio programme "Down your way" paid Debron a visit with the charismatic Brian Johnson asking the questions. But more serious questions were being asked back at Carpets International Headquarters ! The group was in serious financial trouble and, in an attempt to raise some capital, Carpets International was sold to Ray Anderson and his American Interface company. By now, Interface had become a large International company in their own right. Debron was just part of this transfer and Interface decided that all UK tile production would be centred at the former Illingworth Felt Mills at Shelf near Halifax. In January 1983 the *Journal* pronounced "A Question Mark over Debron." but this was only to soften the blow. The decision had been made and one month later the expected "Debron to Close" headline was front page. To observers, it seemed ironic that the Interface company, launched with technology developed by Debron in Bridgnorth, should be responsible for the closure.

Two local MPs took up the fight, Esmond Bulmer of Kidderminster, and Bridgnorth's Eric Cockeram met the directors of CIL and Interface in a last ditch attempt to retain the jobs in Bridgnorth. All was to no avail and in March they announced that production would stop on 27th May. From this point onwards the equipment was gradually transferred and, true to plan, on that day the production of carpet ended in Bridgnorth. It was a sad day well remembered by Debron technician, Jack Childs, who was the last employee to leave the factory some weeks later.

And so, on 27th May 1983 production ceased at the Friars Works bringing to an end over 150 years of carpet production in Bridgnorth.

FRIARS WORKS

With the factory buildings redundant, redevelopment of the site was inevitable for such a prestigious location. And so, Bridgnorth gained a new residential development built by Bovis Homes in the late 1980s and they named one of the roads "Southwell Riverside." However, the foundations of the old Franciscan Monastery caused some concern and Birmingham University were commissioned to excavate part of the site and leave it as a reminder of those former days when "Old Mo" ruled the roost !

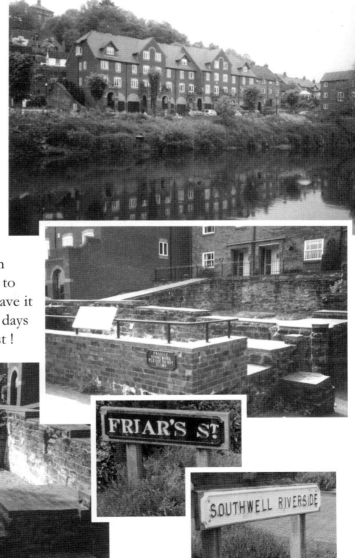

POSTSCRIPT

Interface went on to greater things but Carpets International's carpet business failed to meet the challenge. In 1985 it was sold to the Yorkshire-based John Crowther Group who, three years later, sold out to John Ashcroft's Coloroll empire. Coloroll was large and so were its borrowings. This proved to be their downfall when interest rates move against them in 1990 and the receivers were called in. Kidderminster's Coloroll carpet factories and equipment were sold and the main Mill Street factory site was demolished to make way for a large retail park. However, between 1985 and 1988 the experience gained with the Debron operation was put to good use in a company set up by Carpet International's former Chairman Jim Carpenter. Milcort Ltd. was housed in a unit of the Stanmore Industrial Estate where a small team produced high quality polyurethane-backed carpet tiles for the commercial sector. Roy Delo was responsible for the production and technical aspects.

In the first two chapters of this book Fred Head explained the early days of cloth weaving and emphasised the important contribution made by the Southwell family in the development of the carpet industry in Bridgnorth. In their day they were also pilla of local society, and therefore, it was sad to read of the death of the last surviving member of the Southwell family, Canon Eric Southwell, who died in May 1991 aged 8

Acknowledgements for Part III & IV

I am indebted to the following :- Robert Davies also Muriel Davies and Emily Stennir daughters of Frederick W. Head who provided access to archive material and many of the photographs.
The staff of Bridgnorth Library.
Melvyn Morgan and the *Bridgnorth Journal* for publishing an appeal for information about the local carpet industry and to all those who responded, especially Helen Howell, whose father was the Company Secretary, and Mrs Lowe who donated the "Nitidax" blanket.
Tony Roden, Roy Delo and other former Directors and my colleagues at CMC and Debron who have recalled their experiences, particularly Roy Herring and Graham Sco who were part of the early Debron team. Graham went on to help set up the America company in LaGrange, Georgia, where he now lives.
Jack Childs for his Friars factory recollections and football team photograph.
The Carpet Museum Trust for access to the industry's archive material.
Finally, to Michael Stone of Worcester who cast a critical eye over text of these concluding sections.

Melvyn Thompson. June 200

Further reading : "Woven in Kidderminster" by Melvyn Thompson (ISBN 0 9529937 3 2) also published by David Voice Associates gives a more indepth account of the weaving social structure and the weaves themselves.